With Unveiled Faces

Experience Intimacy With God Through Spiritual Disciplines

Keith Drury

Indianapolis, Indiana

Published by Wesleyan Publishing House
Indianapolis, Indiana 46250
Printed in the United States of America

ISBN 978-0-89827-298-7

Library of Congress Cataloging-in-Publication Data

Drury, Keith W.
With unveiled faces : experience intimacy with God through spiritual disciplines / Keith Drury.
p. cm.
ISBN-13: 978-0-89827-298-7 (pbk.)
1. Spiritual life—Christianity. I. Title.
BV4501.3.D79 2005
248.4'6—dc22
2005010638

Contents

To my wife, Sharon

Who practices these disciplines better than anyone I know

Preface

There are three terms important to the design of this book: *spiritual disciplines,* the *means of grace,* and *spiritual formation.*

The *spiritual disciplines* are those things we do or don't do that bring us closer to God. They are repetitive actions, done habitually, that form us spiritually over time. They include disciplines of action like journaling, prayer, Scripture reading or doing deeds of charity. They also include disciplines of abstinence like fasting silence, solitude and simplicity. However it is important to remember that none of these disciplines have the power to change us. Only God can do that. We cannot make ourselves holy no matter what we do or don't do. We are saved by grace and sanctified the same way—by grace and not by any action or abstinence we schedule in our calendar of devotion. Only God's grace can make us become what we ought to be.

So, if it is all due to God's grace, why practice the spiritual disciplines? The spiritual disciplines are *means of grace*. God has chosen certain channels through which He most often mediates His transforming grace. We call these channels "means of grace." When we practice the spiritual disciplines we put ourselves in the current of God's river of grace. God could have chosen reading newspapers, or jogging or even golf to sanctify us but He didn't. Golf may in fact do the opposite! He might use these things occasionally but they are not the "ordinary channels" of His grace. The spiritual disciplines are these ordinary channels where God provides grace to change us.

This book is about these ordinary means of grace. It does not address the communal means of grace (the Lord's Supper, public reading of Scripture, Baptism, preaching of the Word and so forth). Rather we are limiting our study here to the personal and private means of grace. Occasionally the spiritual disciplines in this book involve other people (like confession or deeds of charity) but even then the focus is on personal spiritual growth resulting from these disciplines. We will leave the corporate spiritual disciplines for a later book. This book is about God and us—and how we might draw closer to Him in ways that change who we are.

So what do the spiritual disciplines and means of grace accomplish? They form us—they are for our *spiritual formation*. These disciplines shape us, fashioning us into an image of God's son Jesus Christ. Spiritual formation is the work of God in His people to make them more like Christ. When lived out individually spiritual formation is the sanctifying work of God transforming us into a likeness of His Son.

The three terms come together like this: You are reading a book about certain *spiritual disciplines* that are *means of grace* through which God can bring about our personal *spiritual formation*.

So what does the title of this book have to do with all of this? It is because of Christ's atonement that we draw near to God "with unveiled faces" and are transformed into his likeness, moving from one level of intimacy to the next "with ever-increasing glory" (2 Cor. 3:18).

Acknowledgments

A book may carry only one name on the cover, but most books are not the product of only one person. Writing a book is not a solitary act. I am indebted to many friends and associates who helped make this book possible. Thank you to Nicole Bennett for serving all year as an able research assistant and advisor from a student perspective. Thank you to Drs. Steve Lennox and Ken Schenck for faithfully reading that very first (very rough) draft and offering suggestions and corrections from a biblical perspective. I express here my gratitude to others who read and revised the manuscript including my wife, Dr. Sharon Drury. I offer special thanks to my students in the Spiritual Formation in the Church and the Local Church Education classes at Indiana Wesleyan University during the 2004–2005 school year, who sharpened my thinking and offered helpful critique as I wrote. Of course I also thank my colleagues and the administration of Indiana Wesleyan University, who winked at my skipping numerous committee meetings while finishing this book. (I hope they haven't noticed that I'm done writing for awhile!)

I want to especially thank Larry Wilson, my editor, who knows how to make me say what I meant to say much better than I actually said it. And to the team at Wesleyan Publishing House, I express appreciation for their vision to make books that promote the formation of the people of God into a holy people. I am sometimes asked why I don't take my books to a "bigger" publishing house. My answer always includes the name of my publisher, Don Cady.

Most of all, I wish to express my deepest gratitude to my faithful readers, who have so consistently purchased my books. Without you, the faithful reader, I could never be a writer.

KEITH DRURY
Epiphany 2005

Part 1

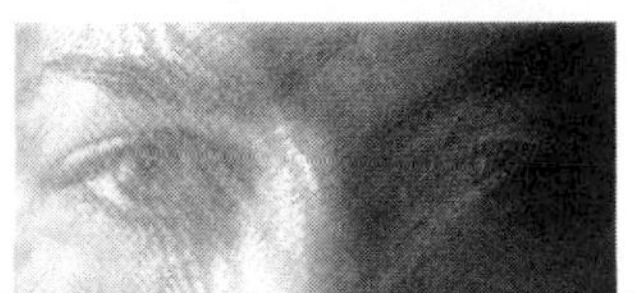

Disciplines of Abstinence

In the disciplines of abstinence, we abstain from things that can distance us from God. These disciplines become a means of grace, a channel through which God can change us as we clear away the clutter that clogs up our path to Him.

Our world is a busy one, and we often feel guilty that we aren't adding enough good things to our lives to make us more like Christ. But we must *subtract* from our lives before we can add to them. That makes the disciplines of abstinence the best place for busy people to begin their journey to Christlikeness. These practices create space in which we can hear God. They also create space in which we can do things—the disciplines of action, which we'll talk about later.

In fasting we abstain from food; in silence we abstain from noise and from speaking. In solitude we abstain from companionship and crowds. In simplicity we abstain from an abundance of material things. In rest we abstain from the frantic pace of work. In secrecy we abstain from taking credit for the good things we do. The abstinence itself does not make us better people. But by abstaining from these things for a time, we get a better sense of God's presence, which changes us.

Chapter 1

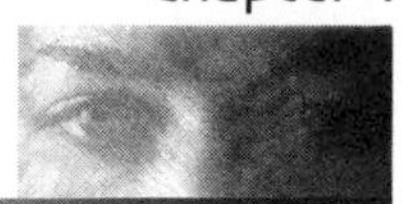

Fasting

When we finish a fast, we cool into tempered Christians strong with self-control. The dross and cinders of our lustful cravings are skimmed off. Fasting produces a work of art—the tempered, selfless Christian—that can be created through no other process of refinement.

Lee Bueno

Fasting is abstaining from food for a time in order to gain mastery of the physical realm and open us up to the spiritual. Christians have practiced fasting consistently through the ages as a way to get closer to God. But even before there were Christians, the Jewish people fasted twice a week and at other set times throughout the year. In fact, people of most religions fast. The idea that we can reach out to God in this way seems to be built into the very nature of human beings. Jesus simply assumed that His followers would fast and gave instructions on how to do it (see Matt. 6:16). He did not say, "*If* you fast, do not look somber as the hypocrites do. . . ." He said, "*When* you fast, . . ." In those days it was assumed that people practiced this discipline, and ever since then it has been assumed that fasting is an important part of the Christian lifestyle. Until recently, that is. Only in contemporary times have Christians concluded that prayer and Bible reading are required but that fasting is optional. Now instead of fasting, we diet.

Fasting and Dieting

Diets help us lose weight, but dieting is not fasting. When dieting, we abstain from food (or fats or carbohydrates or whatever is the most recent fad) in order to lose the extra fat we have gained from eating too much. Diets are about losing weight so we can look nicer, feel better, and live longer. Fasting is about getting closer to God. When we fast we deny our appetite and take control of our flesh. In the process, our spirit gains mastery of other fleshly desires. Dieting can be a good thing, but fasting is better. Fasting provides some of the same benefits as dieting, but adds a closer walk with God. Dieting is a fifty-billion-dollar-a-year business in North America. There is no money in fasting, but the benefits are priceless. What fasting promises is a nearness to the heart of God.

> Fasting gives you confidence to know that your spirit can master appetite . . . and helps to protect against later uncontrolled cravings and gnawing habits.
>
> —Russell M. Nelson

Our Obsession with Food

We diet because we are fat—or think we are. For those of us living in a land of abundance, the concern is not where to find our next bite but how to remedy eating *too many* bites. Our culture is obsessed with food. Eating is a sensory—even sensuous—experience for us. We crave the fleshly satisfaction food brings to the eye or tongue; we even enjoy the feeling of "being stuffed" after a Thanksgiving dinner. The way food looks, tastes, and feels is far more important to us than is its nutritional value. We use food mostly for pleasure. Most preachers and church members alike overlook this near gluttony or dismiss it jokingly. The church usually tries to restrain us from going overboard in gratifying other sensory pleasures, but it seems to celebrate excessive eating. The world is worse. Flip through a women's magazine sometime and count the pictures of food. Men, too, struggle with the addiction to eating as a sensory pleasure. John Wesley wrote of this danger more than two hundred years ago. Early church fathers such as Clement wrote extensively on it. Today few people take these matters seriously, for we have come to accept and approve of this sensuousness. All cultures have evils they pronounce as good. In North America, overeating is one of ours.

> The tempter came to [Jesus] and said, "If you are the Son of God, tell these stones to become bread." Jesus answered, "It is written: 'Man does not live on bread alone, but on every word that comes from the mouth of God.'"
>
> —Matthew 4:3–4

Putting Food in Its Place

Fasting is a way to put food in its place. It is a means of liberating ourselves—even if only for a short time—from food's dominating control. When we conclude a time of fasting, we come away with a different perspective; we see food as fuel for living more than as a sensory pleasure. Isn't that God's perspective on food? Didn't he intend for food to be primarily a fuel for the body and only secondarily as a source of sensuous satisfaction? It is not that we cannot or should not enjoy food—we can and do. There is a time to fast and a time to feast. But periods of fasting enable us to break our compulsive preoccupation with food, to put food back in its place. And in finding escape from the bondage to food, we often gain release from slavery to sensuality in other areas of life.

Jesus and Fasting

Jesus fasted, taught us how to fast, and simply assumed we would do it. We do not have a record of how many times Jesus fasted, but it is fair to assume that His practices matched that of the Pharisees, the most outwardly pious people of that time. That would have included national fasts along with fasting on certain holy days, and, as was common for Jews in those days, fasting two days each week. We do have the record of one long fast Jesus took. He fasted for forty days at the inauguration of His ministry (see Matt. 4). If Jesus—God's son, the incarnation of God—felt obligated to fast, who are we to consider this an optional discipline?

> Is not this the kind of fasting I have chosen:
> to loose the chains of injustice
> and untie the cords of the yoke,
> to set the oppressed free
> and break every yoke?
> Is it not to share your food with the hungry
> and to provide the poor wanderer with shelter—
> when you see the naked, to clothe him,
> and not to turn away from your own flesh and blood?
>
> —Isaiah 58:6–7

There is one confusing Scripture related to fasting, however. Apparently Jesus' disciples did not fast in the same way that the Pharisees and the disciples of John did. In fact, some of John's disciples actually brought the matter to Jesus' attention. (see Matt. 9:14–17). It is not clear whether Jesus' disciples *never* fasted or if they had simply skipped a particular traditional day of fasting. It is obvious, though, that they did not fast on some of the occasions when it was expected. Jesus defends their omission by pointing out that nobody fasts at a wedding feast. In other words, there is a time to fast and a time to celebrate. Jesus' reply is a reminder that fasting as a way of life is not our goal. We should never think that if we could only quit eating, we'd become really holy. If we quit eating altogether, we'd only become dead. Sure, the church has a history packed with examples of radical fasting.

Anthony, an early church leader known as one of the *desert fathers*, lived on only bread and water for decades (bread then was substantially more nutritious than what is available today). But we are not trying to become desert hermits. Few people will read this chapter and then take fasting to excess. Our excess is to eat too much and fast too little. Fasting as a way of life is not the goal of this discipline. We need to know *when* to fast, and *for what*.

Kinds of Fasts

Fasting for the sake of fasting is only a little better than dieting. The purpose for which we fast may contribute as much to the outcome as does the fasting itself. Perhaps the best use of fasting is for *repentance*—for our own sin or the sins of others. This is the sort of fasting "in sackcloth and ashes" we see mentioned in the Bible. When a nation has sinned (or a church, denomination, or family) it turns to God in fasting to demonstrate its repentant heart. It is not that fasting earns forgiveness (nothing we can do accomplishes that), but fasting shows God that we are serious about sin and do not treat it casually. This sort of fast is something like penance and is rare today. When something goes wrong in our family or nation we usually blame someone else, not ourselves and certainly not our own sins.

> Nothing should be taken for granted. We should say thank you every day to God and to each other for all that is provided for us. This is one reason why fasting is such an important spiritual discipline. Not just fasting from food, but also fasting from cars, shopping centers, the news—whatever we have an inordinate attachment to. Fasting can help rekindle our gratitude for all that we have been given.
>
> —Glen Argan

We might also fast to promote the discipline of *prayer*. Indeed, fasting and prayer are twin disciplines, often practiced together. Fasting can cut away the spiritual fat around our hearts, enabling us to focus better on prayer. Fasting and prayer for another's salvation or healing is a common usage of this discipline.

Fasting as a means of *mourning* is so natural that when a loved one dies, those left behind almost always have to be urged to eat. Fasting during mourning also acts as a means of recovery from grief, perhaps even faster than other methods of grief recovery.

There are at least two more good purposes for fasting. One is fasting as a means of *identification* with Christ, as we do during Lent. We might also fast to identify with the millions of starving people in the world. Another purpose is to fast as a means of *escape* from sensuality. The connection between our inability to control our appetite for food and our appetite for sex has long been observed. The discipline we gain by fasting from food can have a spillover effect into other areas of life.

Good Hunger

This chapter is not suggesting that food and hunger are sinful. They are not. The ascetic life is not an automatic route to the holy life. Hunger is a good thing, and eating to satisfy hunger can glorify God. After all, whether we eat or drink we are to do it all to the glory of God (1 Cor. 10:31). But when was the last time we were hungry—*really* hungry. What we call hunger usually isn't. Without knowing real hunger, we never know real satisfaction. One of the gifts we receive from fasting is real hunger. The first bowl of broth after a long fast is far more satisfying than a choice steak. So in a curious way, fasting actually enhances our satisfaction with food; though in the process, it simplifies what it takes to satisfy us. But there is another hunger that emerges: a deep hunger for God. Remember Jesus' reply to Satan's temptation in the wilderness—"Man does not live on bread

> Christ is richer than chocolate, and tastes sweeter than any food.
>
> —Nicole Bennett

alone, but on every word that comes from the mouth of God" (Matt. 4:4). When fasting, our hunger for food reminds us to be hungry for the Word of God. Fasting can make us hungry for food but hungrier for God.

Peacefulness

Fasting can bring peacefulness to a harried life. Our lives are busy. We sprint from one appointment to the next, talking on our cell phones all the way, then rush off to meet someone else. We pick up the kids, drop them off at yet another place, go out for supper, pick up the kids again, then come home and collapse into an exhausted heap. And we wonder why we have no peace. While the discipline of rest has the most beneficial effect on our hectic lives, fasting also brings peace. The discipline of fasting is often melded with solitude, silence, Scripture, and prayer. It is *spiritual* fasting we are after. When we come down from our caffeine and sugar highs, we meet ourselves coming the other way—a more quiet and peaceful edition of the person who began the fast. God uses fasting to transform us and recalibrate us.

> Prayer is reaching out after the unseen; fasting is letting go of all that is seen and temporal. Fasting helps express, deepen, confirm the resolution that we are ready to sacrifice anything, even ourselves to attain what we seek for the kingdom of God.
>
> —Andrew Murray

Dependence on God

Doing without something makes us appreciate the very thing we've done without; in the case of fasting, food. Food is a gift from God. It should be seen that way. Jesus taught us to pray "Give us today our daily bread" (Matt. 6:11). Daily bread is not a sin to avoid but a gift for which to be grateful. This is why we "say grace" before meals—to "return thanks" to God. Even if we earned the salary that bought the food, we thank God for it because all good things come from Him. Fasting is a way to remind ourselves that we are totally dependent upon God. We may think we have greater reserves of food than the sparrows outside our window, yet when there is a storm coming and the grocery store shelves are ransacked in a few hours, we realize how fragile our food supply is. Fasting reminds us that, like the sparrows, we would not have our daily bread if not for God's grace. After fasting we return to the table, saying grace with renewed meaning. God *is* great, and God *is* good, and we *do* thank Him for our food. He is the source of all good things.

> When the stomach is full, it is easy to talk of fasting.
>
> —St. Jerome

How to Begin Practicing Fasting

Start Small

Fasting is like weight lifting. You wouldn't begin weight training by trying to lift a 300-pound barbell. So when you try fasting, start small. As you develop spiritual muscle, add greater loads—that is, longer periods of fasting.

Consider a Partial Fast

A total fast is abstaining from all food and drinking only water. Many longer fasts today are partial fasts, in which we abstain from only certain foods, or liquid fasts, in which we drink only simple fruit juices. Some folk fast from chocolate, carbonated beverages, or beverages with caffeine. You might emulate many early Christians and Daniel, who refused to eat any meat, following a strict vegetarian diet (Dan. 1:12). Partial fasts like these can continue for years or even a lifetime. For centuries all serious Christians fasted red meat every Friday in order to remember the day Christ shed His blood. Partial fasts make the best impact when they are used as reminders, not merely to improve health or give evidence of self-denial. Perhaps you could assign some spiritual meaning to fasting chocolate or caffeine. If you do, it will make for a better spiritual fast.

Start a Special Day Fast

Early Christians fasted twice each week, on Wednesdays and Fridays. Such fasts usually ended at sundown and were frequent reminders of Christ's life and death—sort of like little Ash Wednesdays and Good Fridays. If you were to pick a fast day this week, which day would you pick? Why?

Plan for Next Lent

Regardless of whether your denomination calls Lent by its name or uses some other name like Forty Days of Prayer and Fasting, consider what sort of a fast you might make this coming Lent. For two thousand years Christians have fasted in some way during the time preceding Easter in order to meditate on Christ's suffering. On Easter weekend itself most Christians fasted for forty hours between Good Friday and Sunday morning. Then they celebrated Easter with a great feast, appropriately so, which ushered in a longer, fifty-day period of celebration—the season of Pentecost. What sort of fast might you make for this coming Lent? Is there some family tradition you might begin?

Think about a Major Fast

In time, you may aim to undertake a major fast, for a week or longer. If so, you will want to read far more about fasting than what is contained in this chapter. Some people with medical conditions should not undertake a major fast. Check with your doctor first. In a major fast you will experience reduced energy and the peacefulness you experience may be interpreted as illness or tiredness by your friends and coworkers. People will ask, "Are you OK?" Read more on this discipline before you launch into a major fast. But for now, at least ask yourself if you *ever* might attempt such a fast. Would you?

Now What about You?

What are your specific plans to practice the discipline of fasting this week?

Helps for leading your class or small group through this chapter are located at the back of this book.

Chapter 2

Silence

BS.- 1- -07 Branham.

There is a time for everything, and a season for every activity under heaven . . . a time to be silent and a time to speak.

Ecclesiastes 3:1, 7

Silence is abstaining from sound in order to open our spiritual ears and listen more closely to the voice of God. God seldom speaks loudly. He usually speaks in a "still small voice," often little more than an impression in our minds (see 1 Kings 19:12 KJV). The clamor of modern life easily drowns out this soft voice of God. In the shelter of silence, it is easier to hear God's prompting.

Silence as a Hearing Aid

The noisier our lives are, the harder it is to hear God. We can go for months—perhaps even years—without hearing God speak. It is possible to hear His word filtered through others—friends, preachers, or mentors—while going for a long time without hearing His prompting directly. Some have never heard it. While it is true that God does speak to us through others, He also prompts, urges, nudges, and communicates directly to us. Through the discipline of silence, we seek attentiveness to God's leading. Rarely does He speak in an audible voice, but God does guide us with an inner prompting and speaks to us personally through His Word. We can know for sure that He is leading us. We plan times of silence so we can better tune in to this quiet voice of God.

> Silence is frightening because it strips us as nothing else does, throwing us upon the stark realities of our life.
>
> —Dallas Willard

Devaluation of Words

The more words we hear and speak, the less they're worth. Modern life is crammed with words. We speak thousands of them each day and hear thousands more. Our friends chatter about their weekend, our boss gives instructions, family members talk about sports, neighbors chat about what's happening on their favorite television show. We Protestants have even taken sacred acts of worship like the Lord's Supper and filled them up with words. Our lives are packed with them. But words are like dollars; the more you make, the less each one is worth. Every word we speak or hear reduces the value of the rest. It is possible to fill our lives with so many words of our own that the words of God get lost in the white noise. Practicing the discipline of silence is a way to turn off the many words from our world so we can hear the fewer, more valuable words from God's.

> In the school of the Spirit man learns wisdom through humility, knowledge by forgetting, how to speak by silence, how to live by dying.
>
> —Johannes Tauler

> It is a good discipline to wonder in each new situation if people wouldn't be better served by our silence than by our words.
>
> —Henri Nouwen

Talking Too Much

The discipline of silence involves more than reducing the number of words we hear. It also includes cutting down on the number of words we say. How we love to talk! This is why good listeners are in such great demand. It is the law of supply and demand: there are far more good talkers than there are good listeners. This is especially true in the church. Most Christians "run off at the mouth" too much. The book of James suggests that improper use of speech may be the master sin—the hardest one to control. Proverbs, along with other wisdom literature, consistently condemns talkers and praises those who know how to remain silent. So when we seek silence, we not only "fast" from the voices of others but also discipline ourselves to speak less. This is why (for some of us) the discipline of silence ought to be practiced by itself, not accompanied by prayer or journaling. When we pray or journal, we may merely be talking by other means. More of us should simply zip our lips and quietly listen for God's voice. Sometimes we ought to say nothing unless spoken to. We ought to be seen and not heard by God. For many in the church, the discipline of silence will be a difficult one, not because we will miss hearing others speak, but because we will miss speaking ourselves. But sometimes nothing is the best thing to say.

> There is no need to go to India or anywhere else to find peace. You will find that deep place of silence right in your room, your garden or even your bathtub.
>
> —Elisabeth Kübler Ross

> A man of knowledge uses words with restraint,
> and a man of understanding is even-tempered.
> Even a fool is thought wise if he keeps silent,
> and discerning if he holds his tongue.
>
> —Proverbs 17:27–28

> Silence is the way to make solitude a reality.
>
> —Henri Nouwen

Background Noise

What passes for silence these days usually contains a lot of noise. A motorcycle passes our house. The neighbor's lawn mower has lost its muffler. A faraway truck downshifts nosily for a red light. A train whistles in the distance. An ambulance siren whines across town. These sounds are the background noises of modern life. And to them we willfully add noises of our own, sometimes claiming that our white noise will obliterate the clamor around us. As soon as we get into our cars, we switch on the radio. The moment we walk in the door, we turn on the television. When we invite friends over, we insist on playing background music to banish silence from our homes. We fill up our lives with noise. The discipline of silence helps us escape the tyranny of noise and recalibrate our souls in stillness. In silence we seek to hear one voice—the voice of God. However, there is a catch: the voice of God is usually a silent one. If we want to hear Him speak, we must be willing to wait. The foyer of silence prepares us to enter the presence of the King and hear from Him.

> Only in silence is heard the beating of the heart of God.
>
> —Father Bernardo Olivera

> Be still, and know that I am God;
> I will be exalted among the nations, I will be exalted in the earth.
>
> —Psalm 46:10

Silence and Scripture

The fact that we seek to hear God's voice does not mean that His promptings in our heart are better than Scripture. Almost all of what God has to say, He has already said. Jesus said most of it, and the Bible says the rest. One reason we need silence is to allow God to enliven Scripture to us. God can speak to us by igniting a verse of the Bible or bringing

> He who does not know how to be silent will not know how to speak.
>
> —Ausonius

to mind a scriptural phrase from a song. Indeed, silence is good preparation for reading the Scriptures. And silence is what we should allow following the reading so the Holy Spirit can apply that Scripture to our lives. Silence does not replace Scripture but enhances and personalizes the guidance God gives through Scripture. Silence is also valuable when combined with prayer. How many times have we prayed urgently, then abruptly said amen and scurried away without waiting for God's answer? Practicing the discipline of silence provides time for listening to God after reading Scripture or praying. In silence we listen.

> Solitude and silence teach me to love my brothers for what they are, not for what they say.
>
> —Thomas Merton

Silence as an Alloy

Silence is often used best in conjunction with other disciplines. (In fact, *all* of the disciplines are more effective when merged with other disciplines.) Silence helps us in reading Scripture, journaling, and prayer. Silence is almost always a twin discipline with solitude—usually when we are alone practicing solitude we are also silent. There is, however, one way to practice silence without solitude, but it is difficult to do.

> But the Lord is in his holy temple;
> let all the earth be silent before him.
>
> —Habakkuk 2:20

Silence with Others

We can practice silence without solitude when we are with other people. Holding our tongues when we are with friends or coworkers is harder than keeping silent during solitude. Richard Foster reminds us that a person who takes up the discipline of silence still speaks; he or she simply

> In silence man can most readily preserve his integrity.
>
> —Meister Eckhart

knows *when* to speak and what to say. It is a word "fitly spoken" that we ought to be speaking—saying what needs saying, when it needs to be said, and nothing more. When we flee the noisy life and find refuge in silence, we discover that God Himself is "the quiet type." God often says nothing at all or very little. But when He does speak, His words are always just the right thing said at the right time. We should become more like God when we are with others: saying less but with more meaning.

Silence is the mother of Truth.

—Benjamin Disraeli

How to Begin Practicing Silence

Pick a Time and Place

When could you get away from your normal routine and sit in total silence? Where would you go? Simply schedule it and do it. Or go right now. Don't busy yourself by making preparations or taking Bible resources with you—just find a sanctuary of silence and sit quietly. In Europe many churches are left unlocked for this purpose. You might find a place at your town library, tucked away among the shelves. If you are inclined to the outdoors, you may find a trail or pond hidden away from the noise and chatter of life. Where would you go? When could you do it? Will you?

Displace Penetrating Thoughts

When you first attempt to enter silence, your thoughts may try to shout you down. This is common for newcomers to this discipline. Learn to displace those noisy thoughts by concentrating on one thing, perhaps a Scripture passage or a scene from the Bible.

Find Moments of Silence in Your Day

Try something new this week by refusing to listen to the radio in your car. Or unplug your television for a week and see how the atmosphere of your home changes. Maybe you will want to add "garage moments" to your life: each time you park your car in the garage, sit in silence for five minutes before going in to the house (remember to turn off the engine or you may experience permanent silence!). Even if you have no chance to set aside a full day for silence this week, or even a full hour, you could create one of these moments of silence. Which one seems attractive to you?

Restrain Your Tongue in Conversations

You could decide that this week you will speak half as much as you usually do and listen better. In other words, each time you think of something to say, you might restrain yourself and keep listening (or ask a question) so that you wind up saying only every other thing you would normally say. Watch people's reactions and meditate on what their reactions tell you about yourself. Most of us would be able to go at least one week saying half what we normally say, right?

Use Your Night Watch

Do you awaken at night and have a hard time falling back to sleep? If that happens this week, get up and go sit in a quiet place. Don't read anything. Don't pray. Don't do anything. Just purposely sit in the presence of the Lord. When you get sleepy again, go back to bed. See what a difference this makes the next morning.

Try a Half-Day's Silence

Perhaps you are fortunate enough to be able to spend four full hours in silence this week, just sitting before the Lord. If so, you may experience the greatest impact in your life. Don't try to make this time "worthwhile" by doing too much. The only people we can sit in silence with are those we love, so sit silently with God. He loves you and you love Him. Just *be* together.

Now What about You?

What are your specific plans to practice the discipline of silence this week?

Helps for leading your class or small group through this chapter are located at the back of this book.

Chapter 3

Solitude

At daybreak Jesus went out to a solitary place. The people were looking for him and when they came to where he was, they tried to keep him from leaving them.

Luke 4:42

Solitude is abstaining from people contact in order to be alone with God and get closer to Him. It is fasting from social contact in order to remove others from the God/me equation. The value of solitude is that it closes off many relationships so we can focus on one. Church father Diadochos of Photiki observed that if the door of a steam bath is left open continuously, the inside heat escapes. Likewise, he suggested, spending too much time with the doors of our lives open to other people permits the heat of our souls to escape. There is a time to close the door to other relationships in order to open ourselves to the most important relationship—the one with God.

Fasting Friendships

Friendship is a good thing. So is community. Yet when we practice the discipline of solitude, we forgo the companionship of friends in order to experience a better companionship with God. Solitude is taking time away from others to spend time alone with God. We might survive without friendships. We can't survive without God. Solitude does not reduce the value of our friendships but teaches us to appreciate them more deeply. Doing without any useful thing only reminds us of how much we need it. Absence makes the heart grow fonder, as they say. Solitude reminds us of the order we should maintain in our relationships—God first, others second. A Christian who does not practice solitude is likely to be over reliant on friends and under reliant on God. Solitude corrects this imbalance.

> After he had dismissed them, he went up on a mountainside by himself to pray. When evening came, he was there alone.
>
> —Matthew 14:23

Fear of Being Alone

Why do many of us fear being alone? Is it loneliness we dread? Maybe not, because it is possible to be lonely in the company of others or to experience no loneliness when alone. Loneliness and aloneness are different. In the discipline of solitude, we arrange to be alone with God so that we do not have to be lonely with others. Maybe we fear being alone because we fear being exposed. Solitude (and its companion discipline, silence) has a way of stripping us. Most of us fear being alone with ourselves—we don't like the company. And some of us fear being alone with God—He knows too much about us. We cannot hide from Him. If we do not feel fully forgiven and accepted by God,

> Language has created the word loneliness to express the pain of being alone, and the word solitude to express the glory of being alone.
>
> —Paul Tillich

being alone with Him can be terrifying, like a trip to the principal's office. Maybe that's why some of us cram our lives full with noisy friendships: to avoid being left alone with *the* Principal. But we have nothing to fear in coming alone into God's presence. He is a loving God who knows us better then we know ourselves. Indeed, in times of solitude we can come to know ourselves as God knows us. And over time we can come to accept ourselves as God accepts us.

Community Life

The person who cannot stand to be alone is a danger to a group. Dietrich Bonhoeffer warned us of this in his wonderful book *Life Together*: "Let him who cannot be alone beware of community." After all, what do you bring to any group other than yourself? People who cannot be alone should be suspect to the church. There is something wrong inside them. Is this why there is something wrong in the church today? Are we a people craving community who cannot be alone? It is hopeless to find refuge in community while fleeing solitude. It is when we are alone with God that we find Him—and ourselves—and can thus return to our community renewed and realigned to contribute what we have gained in solitude.

The function of diversion is simply to anesthetize the individual as individual, and to plunge him in the warm, apathetic stupor of a collectivity which, like himself, wishes to remain amused. The bread and circuses which fulfill this function may be blatant and absurd, or they may assume a hypocritical air of intense seriousness. Our own society prefers the absurd. But our absurdity is blended with a certain hard-headed, fully determined seriousness with which we devote ourselves to the acquisition of money, to the satisfaction of our appetite for status, and the justification of ourselves as contrasted with the totalitarian iniquity of our opposite number.

—Thomas Merton

Jesus and the Early Christians

Jesus and the early Christians practiced solitude. Just before Jesus began His ministry, He spent a full forty days and nights in the solitude of the desert. He emerged in power. Even though He had only a few years to accomplish His earthly work, Jesus arranged His life so that He could slip away from His followers sometimes to be alone. Many of the earliest Christians took solitude so seriously they went into the desert to devote their full time to prayer and study. These desert fathers or desert hermits made great contributions to our understanding of Christianity. They considered time alone with God so critical that they gave their whole lives to it. Most Christians today dismiss these desert fathers as wacky extremists. But our excess today is in the opposite direction—spending too much time with others and not enough time with God. When we escape the social busyness of our modern world to spend time alone with God, we enter into the recesses of God's own solitude. After all, God Himself both embodies community in the Trinity and is solitary in His separateness from us.

> Shut thy door upon thee and call to thee Jesus thy love; dwell with him in thy cell for thou shalt not find elsewhere so great peace.
>
> —Thomas à Kempis

Solitude and Self-Definition

In solitude, God corrects our self-definition. All of society conspires to define us in terms of *doing, having*, and *relationships*. In our social interchange we ask, "What do you do?" Or we notice people's possessions and make an estimate of them accordingly. Or we ask questions to discover to whom they are related, then assign labels to them such as "Tim's wife" or "Amber's assistant" or "our state Senator."

> Very early in the morning, while it was still dark, Jesus got up, left the house and went off to a solitary place, where he prayed.
>
> —Mark 1:35

Society would have us believe that we are nothing more than the sum of what we do, what we have, and to whom we are connected. In solitude, God corrects this aberration and assigns a new definition to us based on our *being*. Having a properly aligned sense of self enables us to return to society with purpose and peace and re-connect with our work, our things, and our relationships in a better way.

How to Begin Practicing Solitude

Find a Place

If you want to try this discipline, the first step is to conceive of a place where you might go—a *hermitage*. Do you remember a hide-out you had as a child? Now find one as an adult. Answer this: If I were going to fast from people contact for several hours, where could I go to find solitude?

Schedule a Time

Set a nonnegotiable appointment with God and stick with it.

Keep Your Expectations Sensible

Don't expect wild visions and sparkling insight in a few hours. Just expect to wind down a bit and to sense you are in "God's waiting room."

Keep the Focus on God

It is possible to be alone in solitude without sensing that you are in God's presence. Time alone has some benefits, but time alone with God is better. Work at turning your alone time into God time.

Seek One Important Message from God

If you've not been practicing this discipline as a means of grace regularly, don't expect God to unload everything He's wanted to say to you for years in your first hour together. He is more likely to unfold His words to you over time. At the most, expect only one clear impression each time you slip away with God.

Be Aware of Effect Lag

You may not notice the effect of solitude immediately. The effect may not come for days or even weeks. It may not come at all on the first time you try it. Give this discipline time to change you. Actually, it isn't the discipline at all; you are giving God himself time to work.

Seek Moments of Solitude in Your Ordinary Day

If you decide to skip this discipline (and you shouldn't), at least try seeking moments of solitude within your regular daily schedule. You might follow up this reading by treating your daily commute differently. Or plan a walk by yourself this week. Or after supper one night, go sit on the porch for an hour or two, or close the door to your bedroom for a half hour in the morning and lie awake, alone with God. For just one week, you might decide that every time you park your car you'll take a full five minutes of solitude before getting out.

Try Longer Time Periods

All of the disciplines are not for all the people all of the time. If you discover that the discipline of solitude is a powerful means of spiritual formation in your life, try it for a longer period: perhaps a full day or even a whole week. You don't need to become a full-time hermit to experience the spiritually transforming power of this discipline, but at least try it *some* time.

Now What about You?

What are your specific plans to practice the discipline of solitude this week?

Helps for leading your class or small group through this chapter are located at the back of this book.

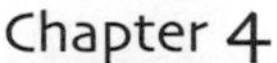

Simplicity

To find the universal elements enough; to find the air and the water exhilarating; to be refreshed by a morning walk or an evening saunter . . . to be thrilled by the stars at night; to be elated over a bird's nest or a wildflower in spring—these are some of the rewards of the simple life.

John Burroughs

Simplicity is intentionally paring down our lifestyle toward the essentials to free ourselves from the tyranny of things and focus more on spiritual life. Few disciplines go more against the grain of our culture yet provide greater freedom than this one. The simple life is easier and less complicated to live, and it enables us direct attention to the most important things. By practicing simplicity, we abandon our preoccupation with the latest gadgets, styles, and must-have symbols of success and embrace more lasting things. In a culture that preaches piling up treasure as the route to happiness, simplicity is our statement of objection. It says that we believe happiness is not found in the abundance of our possessions but in the fewness of our wants. When we practice this discipline, we find the freedom and joy of an uncomplicated life. We come to have a single vision, and our focus is increasingly on God and eternal things rather than ourselves and material things.

Our Simplicity Heritage

Jesus is the ultimate example of simplicity. What were His possessions? Where was His home? What forms of transportation did He use? Gandhi is often honored for his simple life, which enabled him to carry everything he owned in a linen bag. Jesus did not even have a bag. His legacy was a simple, seamless garment—and a worldwide religion. Jesus' disciples took on the discipline of simplicity too. The early church grew as Christ's followers sold their possessions and served others. Congregations sprung up that became known for sharing possessions and caring for widows and orphans. People were attracted to these communities of love in which people acted as if material possessions were not very important. The Christians in Jerusalem did not treat their possessions as their own, and that example typified the early church for several hundred years. The desert fathers denied themselves all the comforts of life in order to focus on their relationship with God. Later, for more than a thousand years, monasteries became places where individuals abandoned the worries brought by having personal possessions and gave themselves to worship, study, and service. Simplicity has a long history in the church and is traced right back to Jesus Christ himself. When we take up this discipline, we join a long line of dedicated Christians.

> Stop trying to impress people with your clothes and impress them with your life.
>
> —Richard Foster

> Reduce the complexity of life by eliminating the needless wants of life, and the labors of life reduce themselves.
>
> —Edwin Way Teale

Temporal Idolatry

> Simplicity is making the journey of this life with just baggage enough.
>
> —Charles Dudley Warner

We might ask, "Shouldn't the Christian life be one of celebration and happiness, not a stern life of denial?" Of course the Christian life is one of joy. Our error is in believing material possessions bring this sort of joy. We are told by our culture that we can achieve happiness by collecting the possessions that typify the "good life." But possessions all turn to dust and rust. In time we discover that we are no happier than when we had nothing. Maybe we are even less happy. We sit surrounded by our pile of possessions yet have an empty soul. Happiness and freedom are not found in an abundance of possessions but in a simple life of trust. The more we possess, the more we will rely on our possessions and the less we will rely on God. Materialism sets itself up as an idol in the temple of our heart proclaiming, "The spiritual world has no value—you can't eat it, wear it, or live in it." To tear down this idol, we adopt habits of simplicity that affirm eternal and spiritual values, dethroning the material. Like a tiny drop of poison added to our coffee each day, materialism slowly poisons the soul.

> Purity and simplicity are the two wings with which man soars above the earth and all temporary nature.
>
> —Thomas à Kempis

Surrounded by possessions, dimness of soul eventually becomes normal. After a while, we no longer even know what it is like to sense the deeper and more important things of life. However, when we intentionally reject the falsehoods of the material life and practice simplicity—even a little bit—we are freed from the tyranny of the temporal world. In the process we become reacquainted with spiritual and eternal things.

Mutiny of Possessions

> Jesus answered, "If you want to be perfect, go, sell your possessions and give to the poor, and you will have treasure in heaven. Then come, follow me."
>
> —Matthew 19:21

We pile up possessions so they can serve us, yet we eventually become servants of the things we own. Our culture teaches us that the material world matters most, so we collect possessions that are supposed to satisfy the soul. Yet we experience a strange disappointment once we have these things. They do not measure up to their advertisements. As a result, we constantly believe that the *next* thing will satisfy us more. This is the treadmill of materialism. But the more things we collect the less satisfied we become. It is like drinking seawater: the more we drink the thirstier we get. Finally, we realize that a strange thing has happened—our possessions have come to posses us. The garage door opener breaks and commands us to arrange for its repair. The lawn mower does not start and orders us to get it fixed. The automobile insists that we schedule a trip to change its oil. We obey. There has been a mutiny! Our possessions have taken over! We are no longer the captain of our ship but have been made galley slaves by our own belongings—we now work for them. We are possessions of possessions, slaves of our slaves. By taking on habits of simplicity, we break free of the tyranny of the material and regain control from the things that have come to run our lives.

> The Christian Discipline of Simplicity is an inward reality that results in an outward lifestyle.
>
> —Richard Foster

Breaking Free

The older we are the harder it is to escape bondage to material possessions. Collecting becomes a habit. After decades, it is a hard habit to beak. When struggling with this issue, E. B. White observed that his house was like a tank with a check valve that allowed possessions to enter but never leave. The valve prevented the outflow of possessions. We pile up things until we move to a nursing home or die. Then our children toss out our junk, wagging their heads and asking, "Now why did they keep *that*?" Adopting habits of simplicity helps us to rotate stock—it gets rid of our old stuff as new stuff comes in. Better yet, simplicity discards possessions without replacing them. When we adopt habits of simplicity, we break loose from the burden of having too many things and experience the joy of traveling light. Sometimes we simply have to walk away from some very large things to find joy.

> To be simple is to fix one's eye solely on the simple truth of God at a time when all concepts are being confused, distorted, and turned upside down.
>
> —Dietrich Bonhoeffer

Frugality, Poverty, and Simplicity

Of course, all of us can't take a vow of poverty—and we shouldn't. The evil is not in things themselves but in our excessive absorption with them. Taking up habits of simplicity breaks that bondage. Adopting just a few habits can do so. The classic approach to this discipline offers three related exercises. First there is *frugality,* the careful use of money in providing necessities in order to get the greatest value. The frugal person gets the best "bang for the buck" or, better yet, doesn't spend the buck at all if the thing isn't really needed. However, as good as frugality is, it is not by itself a virtue. Materialists can be frugal while only saving up more for themselves. Indeed, most misers are frugal. Frugality is good only if placed in the service of generosity. A second exercise is *voluntary poverty*. In

> Most of the luxuries, and many of the so-called comforts of life, are not only not indispensable, but positive hindrances to the elevation of mankind.
>
> —Henry David Thoreau

this case, the emphasis is not on being poor so much as on *choosing* poverty. Some monks make that choice in the form of a vow, actually three vows: poverty, chastity, and obedience (thus addressing three great temptations of life—money, sex, and power). They abstain from personal ownership of anything at all. Few of us could be so radical unless we lived in some sort of commune or Christian community. And even if we did, we still might not become totally free of materialism. Many monks eventually faced a dimness of soul because they merely replaced personal materialism with collective materialism—some religious orders became fabulously wealthy over time. Although the members made vows of poverty, the order owned all kinds of lavish possessions for their use. So even with a vow of poverty, materialism can be a snare. Probably we should all practice some frugality. And a few of us will take a vow of poverty. But every one of us can practice the third exercise, *simplicity*—intentionally reducing the hold that material things have on us by owning fewer things. As we do, we clear away the clutter from our lives, find God, and learn to trust Him better.

> Do not store up for yourselves treasures on earth, where moth and rust destroy, and where thieves break in and steal. But store up for yourselves treasures in heaven, where moth and rust do not destroy, and where thieves do not break in and steal. For where your treasure is, there your heart will be also.
>
> —Matthew 6:19–21

> There is no greatness where there is not simplicity, goodness, and truth.
>
> —Leo Nikolaevich Tolstoy

Relative Simplicity

Where can we find the sensible middle ground on simplicity? We can't all become monks. We have families to provide for, retirement to consider, and other obligations. But how much is too much? How far should we go in unpiling our treasure on earth?

Certainly this discipline must be tailored personally. What would be considered moderate simplicity to a Christian in Rangoon might look like abject poverty to a Christian in suburban Chicago. Living a simple life in North Carolina might seem to be a wantonly excessive lifestyle to a Christian in Bangladesh. Even among friends attending the same local church there will be varying tolerations for simplicity. "Oh, I could never do without that" is what we say when describing what we think of as a necessity. But one person's necessity may be another's luxury. So we will have to apply this discipline personally and be careful of being judgmental about how others live. Most of us feel the grip of materialism and sense our own addiction to nice things. Taking even small steps to reverse materialism's clutch can bring at least some freedom. And freedom breeds itself. Once we start on this path, turning back is unlikely. Certainly no one can set absolute standards for others, but that doesn't mean we do not need to set standards for ourselves. Simplicity may be relative, but it is not optional—at least for the people following Jesus Christ, who taught such radical notions about possessions.

> No one can serve two masters. Either he will hate the one and love the other, or he will be devoted to the one and despise the other. You cannot serve both God and Money.
>
> —Matthew 6:24

Simplicity as Moderation

As with so many solutions, moderation is the key to applying the discipline of simplicity. When we adopt this discipline, we will not, for example, toss out all our clothes and keep only a single change of attire. That may have worked in Jesus' time, but few of us seriously think even Jesus would dress that way in today's world. For most of

> Beauty of style and harmony and grace and good rhythm depend on simplicity.
>
> —Plato

us, simplicity of dress has to do more with *moderation* than *essentials*. If we were concerned only with what is essential for life, then of course one set of clothing would be adequate. But few of us could survive in modern life on only the bare essentials—our world doesn't work that way. The discipline of simplicity moves us *toward* the essentials. It is a journey against materialism that most of us will never complete. At least we won't complete the journey until death—the final downsizing. All downsizing we do before then is only preparation. We will take nothing with us. Yes, we need some things now—probably more things than Jesus had. But how many changes of clothing do we need? How many internal combustion engines do we own (or how many own us)? Two? Four? Five? Do we need so many? Practicing the discipline of simplicity leads us to determine how much we really need and moves us toward having only what we need and nothing more. Taking on this discipline in our modern world is more about moderation than total abstinence. In simplicity we abstain from material excess—from collecting things as if they provided happiness and meaning. Only God can give us the happiness and meaning we crave.

> John's clothes were made of camel's hair, and he had a leather belt around his waist. His food was locusts and wild honey.
>
> —Matthew 3:4

> The ability to simplify means to eliminate the unnecessary so that the necessary may speak.
>
> —Hans Hofmann

Following the Heart

We should remind ourselves that possessions themselves are not wrong; it is loving our possessions that brings danger. The problem is that we can't serve two masters—God and possessions. Jesus said it clearly. He taught us that our hearts follow our treasure. It is hard for the heart to care about eternal, spiritual things when it is caring about temporal, material ones. This is why we practice simplicity—to break free from the mastery of materialism and refocus our eyes on God. And in ridding ourselves of the things we thought would make us happy, we find truer and deeper happiness in Him.

How to Begin Practicing Simplicity

Don't Start Collecting Things

Are you a single person or young couple who owns little more than a stack of CDs, a worn out computer, and two old chairs you got from your aunt? Do you have far more debt than you're worth, and would all your possessions still fit in the back seat of your beat-up car? Then applying this discipline will be easy for you. You simply *stay* simple. You decide now what sort of lifestyle is sensible and determine to not surpass it. Write down a description of your ideal lifestyle and put it in your Bible so you can remember it years from now when you are able to afford a moving van load of things.

Say No to Spending

Pick one purchase every day and say no to it, even something as small as a soft drink. Do this not because buying things is wrong but to break your bondage to the notion that a purchase will make you happier.

Give Things Away

Walk through your house with boxes and take out things you have not used in a year, or two years, or whatever time limit you think is reasonable. If you have not worn a sweater in a year, should you really keep it? If that tool has not been used for two years, why hoard it? Gather a pile of unused possessions somewhere—but don't put it in your attic. Give these things away. Voluntary poverty (a form of simplicity) is not just doing without things—it is a means of being generous.

Have a Garage Sale

Perhaps a garage sale is the way to toss out your extra baggage—having one of your own, that is, not visiting one at your neighbor's house to collect more stuff! Some Christians have a garage sale every year and give the income to support world evangelism.

Get Rid of Leftovers from Your Last Move

Do you still have unpacked boxes from your last move—or even from two moves ago? If so, schedule an hour this week (and every week until you are finished) to sort, discard, or give away those things. Your children will only have to do it anyway when you go into a nursing home. If now is not a good time to start, when will be better? Do you really think you'll be better able to do it when you're middle aged, or retired, or just before you enter a nursing home?

Plan a Backpacking Trek

Most of us are unable to continually practice severe simplicity, as John the Baptist, Jesus, and the early church fathers did. But we can experience it for a short time by taking a backpacking trek. If you are physically able, consider going for a week or more carrying only the necessities on your back. Then watch how what you thought were necessities turn into luxuries once you have to carry them around all day! Let this become a lesson for life. Few experiences today are as similar to first-century simplicity as is backpacking.

Begin Downsizing

If you agree that an overabundance of possessions is actually a burden, then you might take simplicity even more seriously and begin to downsize your lifestyle in a serious way. Give away the extra furniture cluttering your house to a young couple. Or give it to the Salvation Army. Find a young person who has no tools and give away your extra set of socket wrenches—or your only set if you have not been using it. Get rid of all that stuff in your self-storage locker. Why pay rent to store things that will eventually get tossed out? Check the attic, garage, and basement of your house asking, "Why should I keep this?" Give yourself permission to buy things again if you find out later that you need them. Consider moving into a smaller house that will make you downsize automatically. Again, do not take up this discipline because having little will make you holy. Do it because having fewer things will free you to be happier, and do it in order to give to those in need. This act will be a testimony that the spiritual things are more important to you than material ones. And it will bring you closer to God.

Now What about You?

What are your specific plans to practice the discipline of simplicity this week?

Helps for leading your class or small group through this chapter are located at the back of this book.

Chapter 5

Rest

3-11-07 at Most

By the seventh day God had finished the work he had been doing; so on the seventh day he rested from all his work. And God blessed the seventh day and made it holy, because on it he rested from all the work of creating that he had done.

Genesis 2:2–3

In the discipline of rest, we retreat from the frantic pace of life in order to be restored physically and spiritually. The practice of this discipline involves taking days off and vacations, and getting a full night's sleep—every night. Rest is the antidote for workaholism. This discipline is an emerging one that was less critical in the slower paced Middle Ages but is essential in modern times. Christians who ignore rest are often proud that they do, but they pay a price. In rest, God restores the body, mind, and soul—all three of which are interrelated. After the proper practice of rest, we are able to return to a high velocity life with renewed strength, clearer purpose, and recalibrated priorities. Rest is a tune up for us. It lets us unwind so that we run more efficiently when we return to activity.

The Discipline of Laziness

Most successful people fail at one important discipline—the discipline of laziness. Laziness is always a bad word as far as most of us are concerned. Indeed, if sloth is our major personal temptation, then we should skip this chapter completely. But if we are like most modern Christians, we sometimes experience the barrenness of the busy life. We rush about frantically even as we complain about our hyperactive pace. The fact that we are taking life at a furious speed proves to us that we are having fun and doing worthwhile things. In activity we find meaning. At supper we ask one another, "So, what did you *do* today?" We open our Sunday school classes by asking, "Let's go around and tell what we each *did* this weekend?" If we answer, "Nothin' much—I just sat around and vegged," we'll see horrified expressions or hear bursts of laughter. Doing nothing is bad, according to some modern Christians, but doing something—anything—is considered good. So we cram our lives full of busyness to convince our friends—and ourselves—that we are having a good time. By taking up the spiritual discipline of rest, we force ourselves to "lie down in green pastures"—to practice what Lee M. Haines calls "the discipline of laziness" for a time. Rest includes both a good day off and a good night's sleep.

> Sometimes the most important thing in a whole day is the rest we take between two deep breaths.
>
> —Etty Hilsum

> It is a common experience that a problem difficult at night is resolved in the morning after the committee of sleep has worked on it.
>
> —John Steinbeck

> He that can take rest is greater than he that can take cities.
>
> —Benjamin Franklin

Hooked on Hurry

Some of us have a more serious malady; we are addicted to hurry. We rush from one double-scheduled appointment to the next, making a quick call on our cell phone to cover our late arrival. We dash around panting so that everyone knows they should not interrupt us because we're too busy. Someone asks, "How's it going?" and we respond, "Oh, I'm just so *busy*." But we love it. The exciting pace of our lives gives to us the same jolt a teenager gets by speeding over a railroad crossing to beat an oncoming train. It may be dangerous, but it's exhilarating if you live to tell about it. This malady has no cure but one—the discipline of rest. The only exit from the 24/7 rat race is enforced laziness—the setting aside of Sabbath time.

Without warning, a furious storm came up on the lake, so that the waves swept over the boat. But Jesus was sleeping.

—Matthew 8:24

Cease and Desist

The idea of ceasing work came long before the Ten Commandments; it is rooted in Creation. Genesis 2:2 reports that following Creation, God himself took a day off. What a curious claim! Was God so worn out that He needed to catch up on sleep? Why would God cease work on the seventh day? You'd think that if God were truly God, He could work twenty-four hours a day without getting worn out, wouldn't you? Yet Genesis pictures God taking a day off. Perhaps we are told this to remind us that taking time off is built into Creation itself—it is not an option.

The Lord is my shepherd, I shall not be in want.
He makes me lie down in green pastures,
he leads me beside quiet waters;
he restores my soul.

—Psalm 23:1–3

God didn't have to design the world this way. He could have created us so that we need no sleep at all. Without the need to rest, we could work for His kingdom constantly—all day, all night, all year long. How much more

No day is so bad it can't be fixed with a nap.

—Carrie Snow

we'd get done! Wouldn't God have gotten more bang for His buck by creating no-rest humans? We don't know why, but He didn't. He made us as creatures that need rest. Much of the natural world is similar—there is both summer and winter, seasons of growth and dormant seasons, years for planting and years to let the ground lay fallow. For humans, God designated the boundary between work and rest, sleep and wakefulness, and He expects us to budget wisely between them. If we had written Genesis 2:2, we'd have God rushing off after a week's work to water ski all day at the lake then catch a movie before going out for dinner—that's what we call a day off. In the real Genesis, God simply rests. Ceases work. *Does nothing*.

Come to me, all you who are weary and burdened, and I will give you rest. Take my yoke upon you and learn from me, for I am gentle and humble in heart, and you will find rest for your souls.

—Matthew 11:28–29

And rest is more than a once-a-week discipline. Jesus once curled up for a nap in a boat during a powerful storm. Our need for rest is designed into the created order, and tampering with it is hazardous to our bodies. And minds. And souls.

The Sabbath Sunday

Given the fact that God has designed us with the need for a day off every week, which day should it be? For many of us, the true seventh day of the week, Saturday, might be a good day on which to rest. Yet there are so many household duties piled up by Saturday that it may be difficult to rest at home. And if we go away for the day, we sometimes get caught up in "rushed recreation" and come home more exhausted than before. Yet Saturday, for many people, is the day to cease labor. Sunday is perhaps more ideal because the

Sleep is the golden chain that ties health and our bodies together.

—Thomas Dekker

rhythm of our culture calls for reduced work on that day. However, some church's Sunday schedules are so demanding that even this becomes another pressure-filled, rushed day—that is almost always true for pastors. The particular day we choose as our cease-and-desist day is not so important as the fact that we choose a day—some day. The Sabbath principle is a law written into Creation. Making time to obey this law is not legalism; it is survival.

> A good laugh and a long sleep are the two best cures.
>
> —Harry Emerson Fosdick

Rest as a Means of Grace

Rest is God's ordained means of restoring us physically and spiritually. We should not challenge His design. We shouldn't, but we sometimes do. We work continuously, sometimes for months on end, without taking a real day off. We learn to get by on less than a full night's sleep, rise exhausted, and gulp down enough coffee to enable us to function all day. We use prescription drugs to defy the law of rest, yet survive for months or even years. Some college students live a sleep-deprived life, considering it "normal" for four years straight. To be honest, we must admit that we can defy the laws God established in nature. But the payment will eventually come due.

> Sleep that knits up the ravelled sleave of care
> The death of each day's life, sore labour's bath
> Balm of hurt minds, great nature's second course,
> Chief nourisher in life's feast.
>
> —William Shakespeare

Going without proper sleep and regular days off changes us. At first we lose short-term memory and don't remember where we put things. Then we start forgetting appointments and feel drowsy in meetings. We become crabby, irritable, and impatient with others. People start to avoid us and say, "Boy, they sure are touchy." Our minds slowly deteriorate, our relationships degenerate, and our spiritual passion dims. Fatigue leaves us open to all kinds of temptation—and we are not able to resist. When prisoners of war are interrogated, their captors use a standard technique to melt down the captives' will to resist. They deprive the prisoners of sleep. Fatiguc weakens the will. We might seek counseling or pray for deliverance from irritability or weak will. But we do not need to go to the altar. We need to go to bed. God has ordained sleep. It can be a means of grace to restore, refresh, cleanse, and strengthen us. We dare not think we can abuse our bodies without affecting our hearts—they are interconnected. God can work in us while we are sleeping and while we are resting on a day off. Refusing to receive this means of grace cuts us off from God's work.

There is more refreshment and stimulation in a nap, even of the briefest, than in all the alcohol ever distilled.

—Edward Lucas

While You Can

It could be that we resist the discipline of rest because we do not believe strongly enough in heaven. Have we come to believe the old slogan "You only go around once, so grab all the gusto you can"? Do we really believe that this life is all there is—there is nothing more? Have we become practical materialists? Do we fear that the only time we have may be *this* time, these hours, this weekend—and thus we'd better cram our schedules full before our time runs out? Perhaps we imagine heaven (if we imaginc it at all) as the ultimate day of rest and so are determined to do our work now (and have our fun now) because there will be neither work nor fun in heaven. If we do, that thinking illustrates how pagan we have become. But what if heaven is a place of work—without weariness? Or what if heaven is a place of fun—such wonderful joy

He who dwells in the shelter of the Most High
will rest in the shadow of the Almighty.

—Psalm 91:1

that it wouldn't even compare to water skiing or backpacking? What if heaven is like a life of stimulating conversations, wonderful dining, and all the things we now rush to do on weekends? In other words, what if this life *isn't* all we get? Would that cause us to take a less frenetic approach to the coming week? Maybe we all should stop reading this chapter right now and go take a much-needed nap!

People who say they sleep like a baby usually don't have one.

—Leo J. Burke

How to Begin Practicing Rest

Quit Apologizing

Decide to go all week without apologizing for resting. If someone calls on Sunday afternoon and asks, "Were you sleeping?" just tell them yes. If you take a "lazy day" this week, try to find some way to tell others—and do so without any twinge of guilt. When your Sunday school class asks, "What exciting thing did you do this weekend?" answer, "I rested," and refuse to be intimidated by their disappointment. Someone has to break the conspiracy to dismiss God's plan for rest; it may as well be you.

Schedule a Nap

Pick a time this week (or a time every day this week) for a short nap to let God refresh your soul and body. Set an alarm so you won't sleep too long and get groggy.

Turn Over a New Leaf

Feeling drowsy in meetings or during a sermon is a classic sign of sleep deprivation. Most adults require between seven and nine hours of sleep each day. You can survive with less sleep if you are willing to pay the price (and if those around you are willing to pay it too). If you are not getting enough sleep, decide this week—even if only for this week—to get a full night's rest every day. If you are a night owl, you may have to set an alarm clock to *go* to bed—and have the discipline to obey it. Watch how you change, even in one week.

Examine Your Hobbies

Busy recreational activities are not wrong, but they are not rest either. Take this week to reflect on your hobbies and recreational activities. Is there balance between your rest and your recreation? If all your recreation is active, perhaps you should consider balancing it with a more restful activity. If you groan and say, "I can't imagine myself just sitting there doing nothing," you may be addicted to hurry and in all the more need of slow-paced recreation.

Take a Day Off to Do Nothing

Determine to take a full day off this week to do nothing—a day of rest. Set only one goal—to do nothing. Measure your success in resisting work. Submit to God's command to cease work and take a real Sabbath. Reflect on how you are feeling, but not too intensely—that would be work. Don't read or journal or *do* anything at all. Just lie down in green pastures and rest. See if God does anything in you while you are sitting, lying, and napping.

Now What about You?

What are your specific plans to practice the discipline of rest this week?

Helps for leading your class or small group through this chapter are located at the back of this book.

Chapter 6

Secrecy

9-16-07 at Brockman's

Jesus' brothers said to him, "You ought to leave here and go to Judea, so that your disciples may see the miracles you do. No one who wants to become a public figure acts in secret. Since you are doing these things, show yourself to the world."

John 7:3–4

The discipline of secrecy is abstaining from taking credit for the good deeds we do. When we practice secrecy, we arrange to do good things in such a way that others can't even find out who did them. Secrecy avoids getting credit for doing good. It keeps others from concluding that our good works are evidence that we are a good person or a spiritual person. When we take up the discipline of secrecy, we rely on God alone for our affirmation and approval. That strengthens our Father-child relationship with Him and weakens our thirst for human approval. It reorients our "credit compass" to the North Pole of God's approval.

A Culture of Credit

> Secrecy rightly practiced enables us to place our public relations department entirely in the hands of God.
>
> —Dallas Willard

We live in a culture of credit. We are preoccupied with giving credit where credit is due and—more often—*taking* credit where credit is due. Most of our nonprofit organizations have learned that they must give recognition to their significant donors or their funds will dry up. Large gifts are recognized with an announcement or press release or gold plate, permanently advertising the giver's generosity. Everybody gets to know how generous we are. If they could pull it off without appearing too gauche, some Christian organizations would probably arrange to have trumpets sound when announcing great gifts, just as some Pharisee's did in Bible times! It is just how we do things. Because we live in a culture of credit, some of our churches have stained glass windows with people's names on them. We have sidewalks with bricks that display givers' names for generations to come. We screw gold plates engraved with donor's names to just about everything in our churches and educational institutions. Almost every Christian college in the country annually publishes the names of their donors, organized by the amount given, so everyone will know who is most generous and good. Of course, when we do this, we totally ignore the teachings of Jesus. Why does the church so easily dismiss Jesus' clear intent in this matter? Because, as every fundraiser knows, "People won't give if they don't get credit."

> Then your Father, who sees what is done in secret, will reward you.
>
> —Matthew 6:4, 6:6, and 6:18

The Thirst for Recognition

Perhaps the reason we want credit so much is that we aren't completely confident we'll get credit later. We want recognition now because we are earthbound in our thinking. Sure, we know that Jesus promised recognition in heaven, but that is far off and ethereal. Who knows for sure if it will really happen? When a church praises us here and now, we can bask in the honor. Public giving is like a scratch-off ticket—it pays off immediately. Getting credit here is our hedge fund of recognition—in case our later reward doesn't pan out. Being earthly minded creatures, we opt to take our credit now instead of hoping to get it later. This is why the discipline of secrecy is so powerful (though admittedly rare) in the church. Practicing secrecy forces us to shift our focus from earth to heaven and from others to God. Secrecy makes us "bet the farm" on the existence of an afterlife in which God will reward people. If there is no heaven and no God, then we've lost our only chance for reward. This is why secrecy is vital as a means of spiritual formation—it is a potent statement of faith.

But when you fast, put oil on your head and wash your face, so that it will not be obvious to men that you are fasting.

—Matthew 6:17–18

Vainglory

Let your light so shine before men, that they may see your good works, and glorify your Father which is in heaven.

Matthew 5:16 KJV

The desert fathers called *vainglorious* those things we say or do to gain the admiration of others. Vainglory is a kind of vanity, a seeking to glorify the self. Praise from others bolsters our self-esteem. The discipline of secrecy is the cure for vainglory. Secrecy forces us to seek affirmation only from the One who knows us best and loves us most—our Father in heaven.

Now or Then

Jesus said we have a choice of either getting a reward now on earth or receiving it later in heaven. About those who sought credit on earth He said, "They have received their reward in full" (Matt. 6:2).

He taught us that we can actually store up treasure in heaven by quietly doing good deeds and not taking credit for them. If we do our good deeds to get credit here on earth, we will receive no reward for them in heaven. It is our choice—get credit here now or there later. So are the fundraisers right? Is it true that people won't give without getting credit. Is it true of *us*? Or are we better people than our fundraisers think?

In the discipline of secrecy—we abstain from causing our good deeds and qualities to be known. We may even take steps to prevent them from being known, if it doesn't involve deceit.

—Dallas Willard

Motivation

By warning us against taking credit for our good works, Jesus was not telling us we could never do a good deed that others might see. Nor was He saying that we lose all credit from God if we get credit here. He was talking more about our motivation—*why* we do good. If we do good things merely in order to get noticed by others, then we lose our heavenly reward. It is our motivation that makes the deed either praiseworthy or hypocritical. So are our motives pure? Most of us will have to admit that we have mixed motivations. That is, even if we donate money out of pure altruism, when the givers' list is published, we search for our name (and the names of our peers). Taking credit may not be the original motivation, but it can sneak in later. Or our motives might be 90 percent pure, or 50 percent, or they might vary depending on the situation. Secrecy provides a way to purify our motives—and pure motives are what it's all about. When practicing the discipline of secrecy, we carefully arrange *not* to get credit. Secrecy is anonymous giving and anonymous doing. In such

Never desire to be singularly commended or beloved, for that pertaineth only unto God, who hath none like unto Himself.

—Thomas à Kempis

secret actions, there can be no reward except from our Father in heaven. Secrecy tests our motivation. We get no receipt, no thank-you letter, no hug from the recipient, no printed name on a list. Nobody is caused to believe that we are a good or generous person when they hear of what we've done—for they never hear of it. Our friends do not know. Our spouses do not know. Nobody knows. Just God. Is that enough?

> Love [should] be concealed and little esteemed; be content to lack praise, never be troubled when you are overlooked or undervalued.
>
> —Jeremy Taylor

Secret Piety

But secrecy is not just about giving alms to help people; it applies to acts of piety as well. How important this chapter is to a book on spiritual disciplines! Consider Jesus' teaching on fasting. He taught that when we fast we should make ourselves appear as if we haven't fasted at all. It is almost as if He was teaching us a sort of "holy deception." This teaching shows how seriously Jesus condemned spiritual show-offs. What is true of fasting is true of all spiritual disciplines. While reading this book, and when practicing some of these disciplines, we could be tempted to make a display of it. We might be tempted to say, "No thanks. My small group is going through a book on spiritual disciplines, and I'm fasting this week," or, "I took a day of solitude and silence yesterday, and it was *so* empowering to my spiritual life." When we say such things, we might not even notice how we've staked out the spiritual high ground in the conversation. But others notice. The discipline of secrecy extends beyond the giving of money to include the practice of secret piety.

> But when you give to the needy, do not let your left hand know what your right hand is doing, so that your giving may be in secret. Then your Father, who sees what is done in secret, will reward you.
>
> —Matthew 6:3–4

Ironically, we could practice all the disciplines in this book with great success yet be worse off in God's eyes—if we did it only to make a spiritual display or if we became proud of our spiritual attainment. Sure, in a group where others are practicing the disciplines, it is helpful and appropriate to share our stories. Most groups who study this book will do that every week. But putting our habits of piety on display for people outside our study group can waste any gain we've made by their practice. God and a small group of friends will know of our secret piety. That should be enough.

Secret Needs

In addition to secret giving and secret piety, there is a third way some great saints have practiced this discipline—by keeping their *needs* secret. George Mueller is perhaps the best-known example of this kind of secrecy. Mueller founded a string of orphanages across England in the 1800s and started 117 schools where 120,000 young people were educated. Yet Mueller never made known any needs for these institutions—except to God. Mueller directed all his fundraising appeals to one address—the throne of God. Yet more than seven million dollars was supplied over his lifetime. Sometimes the children in the orphanages actually said grace over their empty plates and then, just in the nick of time, someone would bring in food, saying, "We just thought to bring this—what a coincidence." It is no secret that as much as half of the funds raised by some Christian organizations are spent on the fundraising effort itself—and the percentage is even greater for many television appeals. But if all Christian organizations today took Mueller's approach, how would we respond? Would we be sensitive enough to the

> As treasure when it is discovered speedily becomes less, so virtue made known unto man vanishes. As wax melts at the fire, so the virtue of the soul is thawed and runs away when it is praised.
>
> —Unnamed Desert Father

Spirit's promptings to give? For ministries like Mueller's to work, it requires both a leader who doesn't ask for money *and* a people so sensitive to the Spirit that they'll obey His promptings without being asked. Maybe practicing secrecy in the area of need is only for the Green Berets of God's army—those elite troops who really do take God's Word at face value and believe that He will "supply all our needs according to His riches." Few of us place *that* much trust in God. Perhaps more of us should.

> Do nothing out of selfish ambition or vain conceit, but in humility consider others better than yourselves. Each of you should look not only to your own interests, but also to the interests of others.
>
> —Philippians 2:3–4

Exposing and Correcting Our Values

Practicing secrecy exposes the extent to which we rely on receiving positive feedback from others, and it enables us to correct that situation. Without secrecy, we conclude that we are good because others say so. We believe we are generous because we can see our name on a receipt or a list of donors. We figure that we must be good people because everyone says so when praising the good deeds we've done. We believe these things because we keep hearing them. And they may, in fact, be true. The problem is not the truth of these notions so much as their *source*. There is no good thing we can do that will make God love us more. There is no gift we can give to gain His love. He loves us not for what we do or give. Yet He does rejoice when we give generously and do good deeds. He is proud of us, like a parent who posts a child's coloring page on the refrigerator door. But when we seek approval from others more than from our Father, our work is posted on the wrong refrigerator. The discipline of secrecy enables us to sanctify our good acts and gifts—setting them apart for God alone to approve. After all, God's approval is more important to us than the praise of people—isn't it?

How to Begin Practicing Secrecy

Make a List

Start by listing a few ideas for the practice of secrecy this week. Perhaps the easiest way to practice secrecy is to anonymously give money to someone in need—in cash. But think of other ideas as well. Consider how you might do good for someone without anyone finding out.

Create a Reminder

Design some way to remind yourself to practice this discipline in the course of normal life. Put it someplace where you will see it daily and be reminded to take secret action.

Watch Out for Vainglory

Keep watch for indicators of your hunger to take credit. Notice the number of times you think, "Hey, nobody noticed what I did," or, "Why do *they* get so much attention for what they do?" or, "Doesn't anybody care what I do around here?" Use each incident as an occasion to pray, "I know *You* are watching, God—and that is quite enough for me today."

Abstain from Idea Credit

If you are an "idea person," you may be as interested in getting credit for your ideas as for your giving or good deeds. This week purposely avoid taking credit for your ideas. Shun saying, "That was my idea, you know." Figure out how to plant ideas in others, and when they blossom refuse to take any credit for it—even for planting the seed.

Gracefully Take Recognition

If you receive recognition this week for something, take it gracefully, with a short thank-you. Avoid playing self-centered games that are merely contrived to gain greater recognition. Refrain from saying, "Oh, it was nothing at all." Just say, "Thanks." Don't say, "I want to thank all the other people who helped me achieve this." Simply say, "Thank you." Avoid saying, "I was thinking as I heard these speeches that I really don't deserve this honor." Just say—well, you know what to say by now.

Don't Report Next Week

Normally, a group or class studying this book reports on their experiences from the previous week. Skip that report next week. If your group or class wants to know what God has been doing within the group, simply have each person write down on cards what they did—without their names—and then read them aloud. But even that may detract from the effect of this discipline, for then you could all take credit for what was done by the group. Perhaps the best plan is to simply let God be the audience this week.

Now What about You?

What are your specific plans to practice the discipline of secrecy this week? (Do not share these plans with anyone—even an accountability partner. That could defeat the purpose of this discipline.)

Helps for leading your class or small group through this chapter are located at the back of this book.

Part 2

Disciplines of Action

In the disciplines of abstinence, we do without something—food, talking, companionship, possessions, work, or recognition—in order to reap a spiritual benefit. In the disciplines of action, we *do* things—taking actions that bring us closer to God. In the normal course of the spiritual life, the disciplines of abstinence and action are intertwined. But here we are studying them separately. The disciplines of action provide things we can do that open us up to God's work. The disciplines featured in this book are hospitality, journaling, penance, confession, charity, Scripture, and prayer. Taking action in any of these areas does not make us holy, but these disciplines are a means of grace, an ordinary channel through which God's grace can flow to us. When we practice these disciplines, we put ourselves in the way of God's work—and He changes us.

Chapter 7

Journaling

Journaling is not a substitute for prayer but a supplement to prayer, it's a huge blessing to your prayer life because it helps you focus on what you want to communicate to God and really spend time thinking about it, not just rushing through a whispered prayer about it.

Lee Ann, student at Christian Fellowship Church

Journaling is communing and communicating with God through writing. It is turning our thoughts into words and putting them down so we can face them squarely. It is talking with and listening to God without speaking. When journaling, we can pray, listen, study, worship, and confess. Journaling is a discipline that provides perspective on life and helps us adjust our priorities. Journaling is a path away from the emotional doldrums and depression that come from relying on feelings. Journaling moves our spiritual life from the inner ear (where we hear God's quiet voice) through our hands (with which we write) to our eyes (with which we see). It makes our communication with God more tangible. When God seems distant, it is time to journal, for this discipline brings our communication with God nearer.

The Heritage of Journaling

> And you shall write very clearly all the words of this law on these stones you have set up.
>
> —Deuteronomy 27:8

Journaling is a recent discipline, though it has ancient roots. In the distant past, writing was reserved for the elite, who had the time and the money to pay for expensive ink, pens, and handmade paper. Average people did not write through most of history, so the discipline of journaling did not flourish until writing materials became inexpensive and the ability to write became common. For centuries the verbal disciplines of prayer, confession, and the recitation of Scripture formed the backbone of the spiritual life, along with other disciplines of action such as hospitality, charity, and penance. However, once writing became common, journaling flourished, even among secular people, and journaling as a spiritual discipline emerged. Perhaps we should say that it reemerged. Journaling is in fact an ancient practice. When we read many of the Psalms, we are peeking into the personal journals of ancient followers of God. They complained to God, confessed their sins, grumbled about life, and cried out for deliverance. So, while journaling is in some sense a recent discipline, it has ancient roots. When we read these ancient Psalms, we yearn for a similarly open and frank relationship with God. Perhaps we'll find it when we, too, start to journal. We might begin with the Psalms themselves. After a preface on God's law at the beginning of the book, the Third through the Seventh Psalms illustrate how to journal prayers, praise, cries for deliverance, confession, and complaints to God. Then after a short break for two worship-journal Psalms, we get four more wonderful examples of journaling in the Tenth through the Thirteenth Psalms. If we would simply copy the first thirteen Psalms we would learn what it means to be honest with God in

> Nothing has really happened until it has been recorded.
>
> —Virginia Woolf

our own journaling. And we would still have 137 psalms left before having to write our own words!

Time Journaling

> Then the Lord said to Moses, "Write this on a scroll as something to be remembered and make sure that Joshua hears it, because I will completely blot out the memory of Amalek from under heaven.
>
> —Exodus 17:14

Perhaps the easiest point of entry into this discipline is keeping a diary of daily activities—a time journal in which we record where we went and what we did. This "accounting" method of journaling simply chronicles our use of time in the same way that receipts track the money we have spent. Indeed, the practice of accounting itself is at the root of this style of journaling. We will one day be required to "give an account" to God for how we spent our time. By keeping a time journal, we can review the past week's expenditures of time and adjust our plans for the coming week based on our priorities. What could be more natural than beginning a week with a daily planner on our laps? When we see before us the amount of time we actually spent the previous week in prayer or with our children or serving others, we may discover that our priorities are out of whack. We can then adjust the coming week's schedule. Many busy people already keep a time journal in the form of a daily planner or electronic device. But merely recording our use of time is not difficult—it is *reviewing* our time and modifying the coming week's schedule that takes discipline. It is easy to dismiss such journaling as elementary, yet John Wesley, one of the greatest journal keepers in modern times, kept what was like a time journal and allowed many "rabbit trail" ideas to develop from it. There is another benefit to such a review. When we're feeling defeated and we think we're "not getting anything done," a

> The desire to write grows with writing.
>
> —Erasmus

review of the last week's time journal can be encouraging. We may realize that we've done plenty—that we've done some good things, and (considering the week's obligations) we've done pretty well. Reflecting on a time journal each week often brings us to praise God and thank Him for His guidance and deliverance in the previous week. This sort of review prompts personal worship. Time journaling is the easiest way to start journaling. Many who practice this discipline do their reflection each Sunday or at the beginning of each month.

> Write what should not be forgotten.
>
> —Isabel Allende

Being Honest with God

Journaling enables us to be honest with God by confessing who we really are. In journaling we bring "into the light" our sins and desires—our deepest cravings, impure attitudes, darkest thoughts, and angry complaints against God. This is one reason many of the Psalms take a sharp turn at the end. Once things are brought into the light, we get God's perspective on them. Journaling is a means of confession—being totally honest with God. Can we do that "in our heads" or under our breath? Sure. Such whispered confessions work just as well with God, but not with us. A written confession is so much more serious; it becomes more real to us than a mental confession does. So when we journal, we confess—we hide nothing from God. Of course, confessing honestly to God in writing means we have to keep our journals under lock and key. While God is not shocked at our deepest thoughts, others certainly would be.

> I write when I'm inspired, and I see to it that I'm inspired at nine o'clock every morning.
>
> —Peter De Vries

Being Honest with Ourselves

In a journal we come clean not only with God but also with ourselves. We get to listen in on our own confession. A journaled confession ends denial. It has a cleansing effect. It is freeing. Journaling a confession leads not only to spiritual health but also to psychological health. Honestly admitting to ourselves who we really are and what we are really thinking brings continuity to the soul—we become a more "together" person. Coming clean with ourselves improves our relationship with others too. Consider a husband who confesses in his journal how he really feels about his wife's endless prattle each evening, in which she tells him every tiny detail of her day. In his journal he confesses how bored he is, how he pretends to listen but doesn't hear a word, how tiresome it all is, and how he wishes she'd just let him sit and watch television. But in confessing these things before God in absolutely honesty, he discovers a new perspective—God's perspective. As he continues to write his complaint, he begins to shift direction. He reflects on how tired he is and how he's trying just to survive each day. Soon he is writing about how self-centered he can be. Before long, he admits that he ought to be interested at least in a brief report of her day. By the time he has finished a second page in his journal, he is promising himself that he will turn off the television and listen intently to her debriefing for ten minutes each day. Just ten minutes—no more, but it's a start. For this husband, journaling provided an occasion to be honest with himself, then see God's perspective. The journaling then influenced his relationships with others. (I suppose that the *wife* in the above story might make some discoveries in her journaling as well.)

> The true purpose of all spiritual disciplines is to clear away whatever may block our awareness of that which is God in us. The aim is to get rid of whatever may so distract the mind and encumber the life that we function without this awareness.
>
> —Howard Thurman

Journaling Prayer

We can journal our prayers. Praying can be done silently, in our heads, or aloud in an audible voice. We can also pray in writing. When we write our prayers, we give greater attention to the words. Journaled prayers often avoid the "vain repetition" that plagues verbal prayers. They are more to the point and more clearly defined. Journaled prayers can be reprayed over time, and they can be copied and sent to others for whom we are praying. And when they are answered, written prayers give us a chance to record and remember the victory. For most of us, journaling our prayers would be a doorway to a deeper and more powerful life of prayer.

Journaling Scripture

Scripture is another means of grace that combines well with journaling. The entry-level practice for journaling Scripture is simply to copy Scripture word-for-word into a journal. Even this simple act can be a powerful means of grace. When we copy Scripture, it goes through our minds in a different way than when we just read it. In the simple act of copying a passage, we often discover new insights. In copying the Psalms, we come to experience the feelings of the original writer. This recopying of another's journal can sometimes express our own thoughts even better than if we were to write them ourselves. But we can go further than copying Scriptures—though that is a good way to start. We can seek God's word *for us* from Scripture. This is called *devotional reading* of the Bible—searching for God's word to us today from a passage. When we do that, God speaks, usually by nudging us toward the personal application of the passage at hand. If we are journaling, we can write down that inner impression. By writing out

> I will write on the tablets the words that were on the first tablets, which you broke. Then you are to put them in the chest.
>
> —Deuteronomy 10:2

our thoughts, we can examine them more carefully to discern whether or not they truly are from God. The written word is more easily scrutinized. Sometimes we cross out our "first draft" of what we thought God might be saying. When the guidance we receive from God is written down and carefully examined, it takes on far greater authority. If we feel sure that the words before us are truly God's words *to* us, they are hard to dismiss or ignore.

Write, therefore, what you have seen, what is now and what will take place later.

—Revelation 1:19

Remembering and Rejoicing

The greatest value of keeping a journal is the creation of a written record that we can use to remember what God has done. We humans easily forget past victories and answers to prayer. We can also forget the temptations we faced years ago and lose sympathy with others who are facing them today. We can come to believe that we have always been as good as we are right now and develop attitudes of pride and conceit. The Bible often calls God's children to *remember*, and journaling enables us to do that by providing a written record of God's work in our lives. The act of remembering was central to Jewish worship. The annual Passover celebration was a remembrance of the first Passover in Egypt. Most other feast and fast days commemorated God's mighty acts in the past. When the Jews remembered God's faithfulness in the past, it increased their faith in Him in the present and future. Likewise, the early Christians worshiped by remembering the Resurrection—God's mightiest deed in history—and it brought them hope for the present and future. Hope for the future is rooted in the past. As we add to our journals year after year, we collect a potent testimony to God's mighty acts in our own lives. As we review—each month,

The pen is the tongue of the mind.

—Miguel de Cervantes Saavedra

year, and decade—what God has done, we can easily rejoice at His faithfulness. By doing so, we build up our faith for the present and our hope for the future. Perhaps this is why people who journal seem so peaceful. They see today as a tiny slice of what God is doing over many generations, so they know from their own experience that God is faithful. They remember it because they have recorded it in their journals.

How to Begin Practicing Journaling

Decide How You Will Journal

Will you write by hand in one of those blank books, or will you keep your journal on your computer or in some other way? Which method would best fit your lifestyle? Some people journal sequentially, keeping sort of a spiritual diary. Others journal by topic and organize their thoughts for reconsideration and later development. That is especially easy with computer journaling. Pick a method of journaling that best fits your style.

Develop Other Journaling Traditions

Consider developing a family Christmas journal in which each member reflects publicly (to the family) on the past year and sets goals for the coming year. Some churches journal, too, especially new ones. Often, they rotate the responsibility for keeping the journal each week or month among the members, then review the journal as a group at a New Year's "watch night" or other service, rejoicing at God's work.

Settle Security Issues

Never let another person have free access to your journal. Your honesty in your journal will be proportional to its security. You can read aloud or copy sections for others, but never turn your journal loose for others to scan. If you use a blank book, find a place to store it that is completely secure. If you write your journal on a computer, protect the file by password. If you do an anonymous online blog, make sure you password protect it from others. Some great Christians of the past invented their own codes to encrypt their journals. Today, people can use free Internet programs to scramble their journals so they can be deciphered only with a keyword. John Wesley developed such an elaborate code for his private journals that it took two hundred years to break! However you do it, care for security issues so you can be completely honest with God and yourself.

Begin by Copying Scripture

If you complain, "I'm not creative," or "I can't write," then start by simply copying Scripture, especially the Psalms. You may never move on—the Psalms and other Scripture may express everything you want to say in your journal. Why reinvent the wheel?

Forget Perfectionism

If you are the sort of person who frets over grammar, spelling, and neatness, determine to break that habit. God does not take off points for spelling errors.

Doodle, Draw, and Diagram

Sometimes a picture is worth a thousand words. And a diagram can often clarify things better than text can. Leaving some large open spaces on journal pages allows for later fill-in writing, after the thought has "marinated" for a few weeks. Face it, women are more inclined to journal than are men because it is like keeping a diary. However, some men are better at visualizing ideas with drawings and complicated charts or pictures. These men can look at the visual items ten years later and still sort out the meaning. If you are a man, try journaling with drawings, sketches, and doodles to start with.

Avoid Becoming Spiritually Morbid

If you are one of those overly sensitive folk who too easily berates yourself for your shortfallings, make a rule that you will not write more than one negative thing per day in your journal. Journaling is intended to be a means of grace, not a means of guilt. On the other hand, if you are one of those folk who seldom feel guilty about anything at all, you might make a rule that you'll write at least one confession of weakness per session. Journaling should be balanced.

Vary the Approach

Over time develop a varied approach to the journaling methods outlined in this book. Try time-journaling, confession-journaling, prayer journaling and Scripture journaling. Add other approaches as you think of them—let your journal reflect who you are and what you are becoming—it is just between you and God.

Decide Where Your Journals Go upon Your Death

Will you destroy your journals at some point in the future or will you pass them on as a family heritage? Some folk seal them up for a generation and release them to their grandchildren. Others make arrangements with their spouse to destroy or pass them on after their own death. You don't have to decide these matters immediately. But, like making a will, if you wait until you need to, it may be too late.

Schedule Periodic Reflection Times

When would you schedule your "remembering" times? Weekly? Monthly? Quarterly? Annually? Some Christians who journal take an annual retreat—a weekend alone with God—during which they review all their journals to date and celebrate God's great grace so far in their lives. When would you do such a thing? Where?

Now What about You?

What are your specific plans to practice the discipline of journaling this week?

Helps for leading your class or small group through this chapter are located at the back of this book.

Chapter 8

Hospitality

When friends are at your hearthside met,
Sweet courtesy has done its most
If you have made each guest forget
That he himself is not the host.

Thomas Bailey Aldrich

Hospitality is opening our homes, our hearts, and our lives to others in order to develop loving relationships to the glory of God. The English word may sound too much like *hospital* or *hospice* for us to greet the discipline with delight. The Greek word brings out its biblical meaning better. It could be literally translated "lovers of strangers." Hospitality is inviting people we don't know into our personal space and making them feel at home. It is a friend-making skill. Practicing this discipline brings us wonderful new friends, and, in the process, we become more interesting persons. In hospitality we give and get friendship. When we learn this discipline well, it becomes an antidote to loneliness—our own and that of others.

Friend Making

Hospitality helps us develop friend-making skills. When we move, we discover how difficult it can be to break into the cliques at a new church. When that happens, we feel lonely. Or worse, the church may have no cliques! Some churches have no groupings of friends. People attend the services as they would a movie: they watch the show and go home. Churches can be lonely places sometimes. Hospitality practiced in a church helps people make friends. Although the inviting may be done by just one person, hospitality practiced well will spread throughout the congregation and have massive social consequences. Though the Bible commends hospitality and even commands that we show it to others, those who practice hospitality get something out of it too: friends. Hospitality teaches us how to make friends—a skill we need more as we get older. People who have "automatic" friendships because they still live near childhood friends and family sometimes never learn the skill of making friends. As their friends move away or die off, these folk are increasingly left alone and friendless in the world. They *had* friends but never *made* them. Learning the discipline of friend making enables us to move a thousand miles away or enter a nursing home far from family and not be lonely. We can always have friends because we know how to make them. We should practice hospitality because it is right and good, even if we get nothing out of it. But it does produce a significant personal benefit—friends.

> Hospitality is not so much a task as a way of living our lives and of sharing ourselves.
>
> —Christine Pohl

The Spiritual Discipline of Hospitality

Although hospitality brings friendship, this chapter is not about making friends or even the discipline of practicing hospitality—it is about the *spiritual* discipline of hospitality. What makes hospitality spiritual? For starters, hospitality is commanded in the Bible. Indeed all of the great religions of the world insist on this virtue (the fact that some other religions practice it better than Christians do should discomfort us). But anyone can show hospitality. It becomes a spiritual discipline—a Christian discipline—when we do it for Christ and the kingdom of God, not just to have a good time with our friends after church. Just as dieting is not fasting, so entertaining is not necessarily hospitality. Our motive is the test. Why do we invite others over, and whom do we invite? Our motive will reveal whether or not we are practicing true Christian hospitality. The spiritual discipline of hospitality is not just having fun with my friends but includes inviting strangers also. Hospitality adds an invitation to people who are not in my clique. Hospitality reaches out to bring strangers into the inner circle. Hospitality is thus a selfless act. It is done for the other person, the stranger, the lonely person, the new person, and the person who doesn't fit in. Hospitality is unselfish, which is why it is a *spiritual* discipline and why it is rare. It becomes a means of grace as God works through the relationships hospitality enables. God favors working through groups. This is why He left us with a command to gather together instead of a command to engage in the solitary life. While many of the disciplines in this book are solitary, they are not intended to produce a solitary lifestyle. They should lead us back into the church, where most of God's sanctifying work is done. When we practice hospitality, we connect with others through whom God speaks *to* us and to whom God speaks *through* us. Hospitality is a discipline because it is not natural. Naturally we invite our friends to our homes; supernaturally we also invite strangers.

> When hospitality becomes an art, it loses its very soul.
>
> —Max Beerbohm

Hospitality in the Bible

The Bible frequently gives examples of hospitality. Abraham opened his tent to strangers. Jesus was born after His parents were offered hospitality. Mary and Martha offered their home to Jesus on His visits to Jerusalem. In fact, hospitality was universally considered a virtue in the ancient world where desert travel could mean death if local people did not open their homes to strangers. But this practice is not merely an ancient custom designed for eras without rest stops or motels. It is a virtue we ought to practice today. Paul simply told the Romans to "practice hospitality" (Rom. 12:13). The writer of Hebrews reminds us that by showing hospitality to strangers, "some who did this have entertained angels without realizing it"(Heb. 13:2) Peter says we are to "offer hospitality to one another without grumbling"(1 Pet. 4:8–10). John instructs us on how to treat itinerant speakers—"show hospitality to such men" (3 John 7–8). The early church considered hospitality compulsory for widows called to church work (1 Tim. 5:9–10) and for church leaders, too, including bishops and overseers (1 Tim. 3:2; Titus 1:7–8). Perhaps the most startling teaching on hospitality comes from the mouth of Jesus. He taught that at the judgment, some of us will be condemned for our lack of hospitality to Him only to discover that by failing to show hospitality to strangers, we have rejected Jesus himself (Matt. 25:34–40). This is not to suggest a hospitality-or-hell doctrine, but we certainly cannot ignore Jesus' teaching on this point. Hospitality is not merely a nice thing to do—it may be introduced as evidence at the Judgement.

As Jesus and his disciples were on their way, he came to a village where a woman named Martha opened her home to him. She had a sister called Mary, who sat at the Lord's feet listening to what he said. But Martha was distracted by all the preparations that had to be made. She came to him and asked, "Lord, don't you care that my sister has left me to do the work by myself? Tell her to help me!" "Martha, Martha," the Lord answered, "you are worried and upset about many things, but only one thing is needed. Mary has chosen what is better, and it will not be taken away from her."

—Luke 10:38–42

Reasons We Resist

Why are we so slow to invite people outside of our social group into our homes? How come so many of us go for weeks without opening up our homes to anyone at all, let alone strangers? To start with, we are busy. Many of us live at such a frantic pace that we don't have the time to practice hospitality. We might arrange for a quick meal at a restaurant or an evening at the movies, but we simply don't have time to invite people into our homes. There is another reason though. If we invite our friends or our small group over and add a few newcomers to the mix, our friends may wonder, "What are *they* doing here?" Most of us like stable cliques or small groups, so if we let our natural selves rule, we will fellowship only with those we already know and like. Inviting strangers into our cliques and groups makes our friends feel awkward, so we don't even try.

> Hospitality in the prairie country is not limited. Even if your enemy passes your way, you must feed him before you shoot him.
>
> —O. Henry

Hospitality versus Entertainment

If we feel compelled to do something elaborate whenever people come to our homes, we may not be practicing true hospitality. Rushing home to perfectly clean up the house and arrange an impressive meal could indicate that we are more concerned about impressing people than in being hospitable. Hospitality is about the guest, not the host. It does not focus on the host's skill at making fancy preparation or immaculate housekeeping but on answering this question: "What will make people feel a part of our family?" Being a fancy host who entertains elaborately can be merely a way to gather an audience for oneself. Hospitality is inviting. It invites people in, not to become an audience but to experience our family life. The best hospitality makes strangers feel at home. It makes guests want to kick off their shoes and put on slippers.

Our Example

God is the original Host, of course. He extended an invitation to us when we were strangers—even enemies—to come into His family. He desires a relationship with us and calls us to himself. God is the shepherd-host who prepares a table before us. At His final meal on earth, the Lord's Supper, Jesus promised that we would one day join Him at another meal—the Marriage Supper of the Lamb. God has invited us into the warmth of His family. Now He asks us to do likewise, inviting others into our homes. God is hospitable. Hospitality is godly. Practicing the discipline of hospitality makes us more like God.

Men and Hospitality

Hospitality is sometimes wrongly considered a feminine virtue. Men are not exempt from the call to hospitality. A man's personal space might be the garage, yard, or hunting lodge, but men can still be inviting of strangers. Men practice hospitality when they call a neighbor to their garage to help unload the lawn mower rather than insisting on doing it themselves. When a man invites a couple of strangers along with his friends to watch *Monday Night Football*, he is practicing hospitality. Men practice hospitality when they invite an outsider to join their buddies on the annual hunting trip. Hospitality opens our personal space and our lives to other people, especially strangers, in order to develop relationships with them. Men should do this just as much as women should. Some just do it differently.

Hail Guest! We ask not what thou art;
If Friend, we greet thee; hand and heart;
If Stranger, such no longer be;
If Foe, our love shall conquer thee.

—Arthur Guiterman

Third Step Hospitality

The first step in hospitality is inviting friends into our personal space. But what credit is it that we show hospitality to the people we like? Not much—this is the sort of things even pagans do. It is not wrong to invite friends over, but it is not the spiritual discipline of hospitality. If we need discipline to spend time with our friends, we probably need therapy! The spiritual discipline of hospitality goes a second step: inviting strangers, outsiders, foreigners, and outcasts into our lives. This is why it is a *discipline*—it isn't normal behavior for self-centered people and self-protecting cliques to reach out to strangers. So second-step hospitality is inviting strangers along with friends. There is a third step to hospitality, however, and Christians take it. At least the serious ones do. Third-step hospitality is inviting *enemies* into our lives. This step brings an enemy into our personal space in order to build or heal a relationship. It is hard to eat with an enemy. Either an enemy will destroy the meal or the meal will destroy the enemy. Christians destroy their enemies by making them friends. Eating together melts icy relationships, heals hurting wounds, and cures smoldering anger. Either that will happen or the person will walk away. Hospitality forces a resolution. Eating together is sacred, perhaps even a means of grace when taken as such. That may be one reason Jesus established a communal meal—the Eucharist—as a tangible reminder of His death and the core element of worship. Eating brings people

> Then the King will say to those on his right, "Come, you who are blessed by my Father; take your inheritance, the kingdom prepared for you since the creation of the world. For I was hungry and you gave me something to eat, I was thirsty and you gave me something to drink, I was a stranger and you invited me in, I needed clothes and you clothed me, I was sick and you looked after me, I was in prison and you came to visit me."
>
> —Matthew 25:34–36

together. So, are we ready for third-step hospitality: inviting an enemy for dinner? Could we invite some people who are estranged from our church to the next party? They could say no, of course. But the discipline of hospitality is not about what *they* do. It is about what *we* do. Most of Christ's church needs to move toward second-step hospitality—inviting strangers along with our friends. And a few of us should feel compelled to go the third step—showing hospitality to our enemies.

Communal Hospitality

This book focuses on personal disciplines, but we should at least be aware that there is such a thing as *communal hospitality*. A group can be either hospitable or inhospitable, just like an individual. Hospitality for a church is making room for outsiders and turning them into insiders. Some churches are simply inhospitable places. They claim, "We're a loving church—just like a family." What they don't add is this: "In fact, this church *is* a family and nobody else can break into our close-knit circle!" It is possible for a church to be a loving place for the people already in the club yet be inhospitable to outsiders. When we practice hospitality as a church, we warmly welcome newcomers. We scoot down the pew to make room for visitors so they don't have to clamber over our knees to find a seat. We encourage new folk to lead a discussion in Sunday school or serve as ushers. Hospitable churches make newcomers feel at home. And the newcomers stay because after just a few weeks, they consider the new church to be their home. All churches get rid of strangers. Inhospitable churches get rid of strangers by cold-shouldering them away. Hospitable churches get rid of them by making them friends. When we practice hospitality at church, we are being like God, for He invited us into His family when we were His enemies. Of all places, the church should be the most hospitable.

How to Begin Practicing Hospitality

Offer a Guest Room to the Church

Offer your guest room to future speakers or college groups who might need a place to stay when coming to your church. The use of motel lodging for guest speakers is a great time saver for the church, but it often banishes the speaker to a lonely life in a sterile atmosphere. Inviting a guest into your home will enrich your life, and, if you have children, it will immensely affect their future. Don't "entertain" your guests to death or dump your problems on them. In fact, don't even spend too much time "picking their brains" for a good idea. Let them rest just as they would at their own home—this is hospitality.

Feed the Birds

OK, it sounds silly. But perhaps hospitality could begin by feeding the birds or even those bothersome squirrels in your neighborhood. If you're the kind of person who'd rather shoot animals than welcome them, perhaps that attitude bleeds over into your relationships with people. If so, learn to be more welcoming to the animal "trespassers" at your home, and you may become more welcoming to the human interlopers in your life. If you start with the birds, you can move up to people later!

Invite Neighbors over Some Night This Week

How long have you lived where you now live? Have you had your neighbors into your home yet? Have you invited them for a meal? Invite one neighbor this week—not for a whole evening with fancy fixings—just send out for pizza and get to know them. At least get them inside your personal space.

Open Your Home to the Youth Group

Youth groups are always looking for new places to go. Offer your house, yard, or barn to the youth leaders in your church—and decide ahead of time you won't walk around and do damage assessment when they leave.

Invite a Single or Married Person to Your Home

If you are married, invite a single person to your home. If single, invite a married couple. Find someone whose family situation is different from yours and include them in what you are doing. Who knows? Maybe you'll make a new friend.

Add Someone to Your Holiday Invitation List

Can you think of anyone who might be alone this Thanksgiving or Christmas? Why not invite them to join you for the holiday? You wouldn't lose much, and they'd gain a whopping lot. If you were to do this, whom would you invite?

Bring a Beggar Home for Dinner

If you never see beggars, forget this one. But if you happen to see a hungry person this week, why not risk enough to bring them home for dinner before sending them on their way. Some have entertained angels by doing this. Why not you?

Now What about You?

What are your specific plans to practice the discipline of hospitality this week?

Helps for leading your class or small group through this chapter are located at the back of this book.

Chapter 9

Confession

Therefore confess your sins to each other and pray for each other so that you may be healed. The prayer of a righteous man is powerful and effective.

James 5:16

The spiritual discipline of confession is humbly admitting our sins and shortcomings to another person as a means of spiritual healing. Of course we should confess first to God in prayer. But the spiritual discipline of confession is not about confessing to God in solitude but about confessing to another person in community. Confession is good for the soul. The act of confessing is humbling. It prevents us from casting an image that is better than we really are. Confessing our sins to one another lets others "see through us." In confession we become transparent. We make known to others what God already knows. Of course, another person cannot forgive our sin—only God can do that. But another person who serves as a *confessor* can represent God in affirming that we are indeed forgiven. Thus, confession can bring assurance of forgiveness to us. There is no stronger vice than a hidden vice. Confessing our sins and temptations before another person weakens sin's hold on us. While most of the other spiritual disciplines are conducted in private, this one requires another person. Confession is an interpersonal spiritual discipline that produces significant personal gains. It produces enormous psychological benefits as well.

The Desire for Privacy

Why not keep our sins and faults just between God and us? Why get others involved? Nobody can forgive sin but God—there is only one mediator between God and mankind, Christ Jesus. But the Bible calls us to go beyond private confession to God alone. It says, "Confess your sins to each other" (James 5:16). What right do we have to dismiss this command? Christians are supposed to find other Christians and make a full confession to them. It is the Bible's way. Certainly we ought to confess to God first, but then we should finish the work by finding another person or a small group with whom to complete our confession. Why is this so hard to obey? Perhaps it is because of the second half of a well-known quote: "Confession is good for the soul—but bad for the reputation." The point of the quote is to remind us that keeping our confession between God and us is safer in terms of our reputation with others. Confessing to someone else would give that person a glimpse of who we really are. It could harm our carefully manicured reputation. That is why confession is the most powerful antidote to the nastiest sin of all—pride. We don't have to confess everything to everybody, but we certainly ought to confess some things to somebody. The Bible tells us to.

> They stood where they were and read from the Book of the Law of the Lord their God for a quarter of the day, and spent another quarter in confession and in worshiping the Lord their God.
>
> —Nehemiah 9:3

The Benefits of Confession

The fact that the Bible commands confession should be reason enough for us to do it. But there are benefits beyond obedience. Confession is a humbling experience, so when we do it, we increase the virtue of *humility* within ourselves. Confession opens the door to feeling forgiven. We may have long ago confessed our sins to God yet still feel a tinge of guilt. Why? Because *being* forgiven and *feeling* forgiven are two different things. We can be forgiven in a moment by God yet continually carry a sense of guilt. When we confess to others, see their forgiving attitude, and hear their pronouncement that God has indeed forgiven us, we often find the assurance of forgiveness that we crave. Feeling forgiven makes it easier to forgive ourselves.

> When this became known to the Jews and Greeks living in Ephesus, they were all seized with fear, and the name of the Lord Jesus was held in high honor. Many of those who believed now came and openly confessed their evil deeds. A number who had practiced sorcery brought their scrolls together and burned them publicly. When they calculated the value of the scrolls, the total came to fifty thousand drachmas.
>
> —Acts 19:17–19

Confession also provides *accountability*. Each of us will someday give an account of ourselves before God. Confession lets us make an accounting before a confidant here on earth. When we have confessed our sins and temptations to another person, we give that person permission to correct and caution us. Confession connects us with others and makes our temptations and sins their business too. It gives them permission to watch us, nudge us, remind us, and even reprove us.

The greatest benefit of confession may be the *healing power* we receive from doing it. Confession has a curative effect. This is why James finishes his statement about confession with a word about healing. He writes, "Confess your sins to each other and pray for each

> An implicit confession is almost as bad as an implicit faith; wicked men commonly confess their sins by wholesale. We are all sinners; but the true penitent confesses his sins by retail.
>
> —Thomas Brooks

other *so that you may be healed*" (James 5:16, emphasis added). There is both physical and spiritual healing in owning up to our sins and temptations. It heals our wounds. It makes us better and stronger. It helps us recover. This curative effect of confession is central to all twelve-step recovery programs. In step four, people make "a searching and fearless moral inventory" of their life, confessing their true state. A chain of addictive behavior is often connected to hidden past resentments. There is healing and freedom in bringing others into the quiet sanctuary of our lives, making a full confession to them, then receiving their affirmation that God has indeed completely forgiven us.

Confession in the Early Church

This spiritual discipline is a hard one for Protestants to accept. We conjure up an image of Catholics lined up at the confessional where a priest waits to dispense forgiveness. We complain, "But only God can forgive sins!" We would rather keep our sins between God and us, naturally. So while we recognize that the Bible urges us to confess, we are slow to obey. But our mental image of confession only shows our ignorance of Christian history. For one thing, even in the Roman Catholic church, the priest does not "dispense forgiveness." Also, confession was never a strictly Catholic rite. Confession as a ritual appeared fairly early in the church and took its place in weekly worship long before the emergence of the Roman church. Actually, at the very beginning, the church had no provision whatsoever for dealing with sin after a person was baptized—it was simply assumed that sin was gone forever once a person entered the kingdom of God. Experience taught otherwise, however. The church rapidly responded with two rituals that dealt with sin after baptism: confession and penance. Making confession a ritual (as opposed to a spiritual discipline) is not without problems. It is easy to get on the sin-and-confess treadmill. Henry Ward Beecher once remarked, "There are many persons who look on Sunday as a sponge to wipe out the sins of the week." The Christian life hopes for more than such a weekly emptying of the trash. Penance was added to confession by the 300s so that a person would have to do more than simply confess sin and walk away. Penance was supposed to train them to stop sinning. Eventually the church specified precise acts of penance for certain sins, just as the laws of every country in the world now do. So confession has been a part of the church from its early stages.

Luther and Calvin

Through the Middle Ages, confession was corrupted and even used in fundraising schemes along with other rites and sacraments of the church. In the 1500s the Reformer Martin Luther rejected the idea that a person was *required* to make confession to a priest, but Luther was deeply convinced that making confession to a priest was a means of grace for believers. The Protestants, as those who accepted the Reformers' ideas became known, believed that all believers are priests and it was therefore possible to make confession to any other believer. The "priesthood of believers" did *not* mean that a person could serve as his or her own priest, as many assume now. It meant that any other believer—not just a member of the clergy—could serve as a priest and hear confessions. John Calvin, another Reformer, also opposed compulsory confession but valued private confession because he saw how it brought assurance of sins forgiven. However, Calvin preferred that pastors serve as the confessors for their people.

> The confession of evil works is the first beginning of good works.
>
> —Augustine

John Wesley and Confession

Because John Wesley is well known for his teaching on sanctification and holiness, one might think he'd have little to say about confession. What would a holy people confess? However, the opposite is true of John Wesley. In the 1700s he took this spiritual discipline more seriously than any Protestant before and perhaps since. In weekly small group sessions called *class meetings*, the Methodists were instructed to "speak freely and plainly about the true state of their souls." While Wesley taught the possibility of living a holy life, he did not ignore the need for confession. In his meetings four questions of accountability were to be asked of each person every week—

"What known sins have you committed since our last meeting?"

"What temptations have you met with?"

"How were you delivered?"

"What have you thought, said, or done of which you doubt whether it be sin or not?"

Do you know of many Christians today—even Wesley's heirs, those in the Holiness Movement—who risk facing such questions among their peers each week? While some cell groups and accountability groups take confession as seriously as Wesley did, it is rare. Imagine going around the circle one by one in a small group confessing every sin we are aware of committing since the last meeting. If we have not knowingly sinned, certainly we have been tempted—so we would talk about those temptations and precisely how we were delivered from sinning. Finally,

But if they will confess their sins and the sins of their fathers—their treachery against me and their hostility toward me, which made me hostile toward them so that I sent them into the land of their enemies—then when their uncircumcised hearts are humbled and they pay for their sin, I will remember my covenant with Jacob and my covenant with Isaac and my covenant with Abraham, and I will remember the land.

Leviticus 26:40–42

we would submit to the group's spiritual leaders by reporting anything we have thought, said, or done of which we're unsure whether it is sin or not—then the group would help us decide if it was sin (moderating the too-sensitive conscience or the seared conscience). Most of us who live in a world where spirituality has been privatized and secretized cannot imagine following John Wesley's approach. We say, "It's none of their business!" or, "That's between me and God." Most of us would be terrified of doing this sort of confession with a group of twelve people. But could we do it with one?

> Hearing nuns' confessions is like being stoned to death with popcorn.
>
> —Fulton J. Sheen

Confession and Us

Martin Luther, John Calvin, and John Wesley were then—this is now. They were themselves, and we need to be ourselves. So do *we* need confession now? If so, how? Certainly a counseling setting provides a good format for some confession. In fact, pastoral counseling and friendship counseling may be the dominant settings in which we confess today. Many Protestants don't know that the traditional confession booth of the Roman Catholic church has largely been replaced by what is now called the *sacrament of reconciliation*—something more like face-to-face therapeutic counseling than the veiled confessional we see in old movies. But still, fewer Catholics today confess by either mode. And very few Protestants confess at any time.

Could it be that we take confession less seriously today because we now take sin less seriously? Yet God takes sin seriously, and we should too. So we should confess—both to God and to someone else. Some worship liturgies include a generic, weekly confession in which we admit as a group, "We have done things we ought not to have done and left undone things we ought to have done." That helps, and may open us up to practicing personal confession more consistently. But the practice of specific and personal confession is rare outside of a scattering of accountability groups and small groups. Perhaps it is time to restore confession to Protestant circles. Then we'd see more of the humility, release, healing, and liberation it supplies.

What to Confess

There is more to confess than sin. We have spoken mostly of confessing sin but there is much more to confess to your confidant/confessor when you get one. Here are some things to confess.

Recent Purposeful Sin. Sin is like a fire in that it can be quenched at first with a glass of water, but left to itself, it will consume the whole house. Confessing recent sin cuts a firebreak across the path of spreading sin.

Recent Unintentional Sin. Even if our intentions are perfect, we sometimes sin against one another and don't know it until it is pointed out. We become accountable for these sins once we know about them, and they should be confessed. Often, sins of the tongue are in this category.

Sins of Attitude. Inner attitudes in the recesses of our heart, like bitterness, grudges, ill will, envy, racism, jealousy, or resentment, should be confessed.

To confess a fault freely is the next thing to being innocent of it.

—Publilius Syrus

Recent Temptations. What sin is Satan enticing us toward? What sinful attitudes could grow if we don't weaken their hold by bringing them into the light?

Past Sins. Even if they are long ago forgiven, if we still sense some level of guilt for past sins, we may need to confess them to another to bring final inner healing.

Flaws and Faults. Even though they are not sin, flaws and faults can still block our spiritual effectiveness. So we confess things like being too self-centered, talking too much, being too-easily hurt, being lazy, overly sensitive, harsh, or other tendencies that could lead to sin or make us less effective.

Can we imagine what regular confession of this sort would do for us? Think of the change that would come over a church body that did what we are all supposed to do—confess sins one to another. Why do we linger and delay? This would be a great week to start the discipline of confession and get in the flow of God's grace through this channel.

> Confessed faults are half-mended.
>
> —Scottish Proverb

How to Begin Practicing Confession

Confess Something This Week to Someone

Even if you do not take this chapter very seriously, at least confess one thing to someone this week—even if you consider it only homework for this book. Come clean about one thing to a coworker, friend, or spouse. Perhaps you aren't attracted to high-grade confession, but you could do something low grade couldn't you? Do you feel you have nothing to confess? Then ask your roommate, spouse, or children for suggestions.

Be Careful of Broadcasting Confessions

Sensing full forgiveness from others sometimes leads an immature person to confess too broadly. Confession is not advertising. It is not designed to tell everybody your tawdry sins in order to "give them something to talk about." It is for you—so you can be humbled and assured of God's grace and forgiveness. The circle of confession seldom needs to be larger than the circle of offense.

Think of Someone Who Could Become a Personal Confessor

To whom would you go if you wanted to confess something? Whom could you trust to keep things secret? Who would have the grace to hear your confession forgivingly? Who would have the wisdom to guide you and the authority to assure you that God has indeed (perhaps long ago) forgiven you on the basis of the death of Jesus Christ? Can you think of such a person? Would it be a pastor or a layperson? Someone near or far away? Someone you already know or a stranger you've heard about? If you are to begin this discipline, you will need someone to whom you can confess—the first step is thinking of who that might be.

Talk with Your Prospective Confessor

When you find a person in whom you'd like to confide, tell that person what you want to do. Show this chapter to the person and ask if he or she is willing to hear your confession and assure you of God's grace.

Start Small

Although you may trust your confidant/confessor, start small. Review the list above, and start with your flaws and faults before working up to recent sin. Don't worry; as you find the joy of true confession, you'll then be motivated to move deeper on the list.

Accept God's Word through Your Confessor

Just as you allow God to speak to you through your preacher, let Him speak through your confessor—this is the best understanding of the concept of the priesthood of all believers. Listen for God's assurance that you are forgiven, and believe it. You may have to help your confessor understand that you aren't looking for advice so much as assurance. Good advisors are often poor confessors. What you need is a listening ear, an accepting smile, a gentle spirit, a nodding head, kind eyes, empathetic facial gestures, and a person who will speak God's words into your life and then pray without giving you advice.

Now What about You?

What are your specific plans to practice the discipline of confession this week?

Helps for leading your class or small group through this chapter are located at the back of this book.

Chapter 10

Scripture

The Bible is the truest utterance that ever came by alphabetic letters from the soul of man, through which, as through a window divinely opened, all men can look into the stillness of eternity, and discern in glimpses their far-distant, long-forgotten home.

Thomas Carlyle

Scripture as a spiritual discipline is reading, studying, memorizing, meditating upon, and obeying the Bible in order to know God and become more like Him. Scripture is perhaps the primary personal spiritual discipline in use today and is usually practiced by means of the modern habit of having "personal devotions," where it is combined with prayer. Scripture is not the oldest spiritual discipline (prayer has been around much longer), but since the Reformation, it has become the most important one for Protestants. In Scripture we find the story of God and His people. Here we discover God's values, commands, and character, and we discover what He expects from us. The Bible was not given primarily to tell us how to live but to show us who God is—for once we truly know who God is, we will know how to live.

While the Bible demands a particular lifestyle, Scripture is more than a collection of rules. It is the story of God. God is the primary subject of the Bible. It is His-story.

The Word in the Word

The very best way to get to know God is to get to know Jesus. Jesus is the Revelation of God—He came to show us who God is. Thus, we Christians should especially focus our attention on the four Gospels, for there we find "God in Christ Jesus." God did not send the Bible to die for our sins; He sent His Son, Jesus. We do not worship the Bible but Jesus Christ. The Word of God is Christ, but the Bible is our record of this Word. The Bible is precious to us. How would we know of Jesus Christ if we had no Scripture? All of Scripture is inspired—Leviticus, Ezra, Hebrews, and Jude, along with the Gospels, where we find the Revelation of God, Jesus. Thus we read the whole Bible, not just the Gospels. But as Christians (and as the Christian church), we make the Gospels central to our reading because the incarnation, life, death, and resurrection of Jesus Christ the Son of God are central to our faith. This is why we call ourselves *Christ*ians.

How Scripture Changes Us

Words are powerful. They can cause people to like us or hate us. They can incite persecution, racism, violence, or war. They can also rouse compassion, tenderness, or understanding and bring peace. The capacity to use words may be the most powerful capability God has granted to us. Perhaps he did so because we are created in His own image. Used properly, words can be used by parents to send their child in the right direction in life. Used wrongly, words can cause wounds from which a child may spend a lifetime recovering. Words are pilgrims as they pass

> Sanctify them by the truth; your word is truth.
>
> —John 17:17

through our ears but become permanent settlers in our heads and hearts. If our own human words have this much power, imagine the power of God's words. As God's words pass through our ears and take residence inside us, we are changed. Over time we become what we see, hear, and say. When we practice the spiritual discipline of Scripture, we begin to "think like God." We come to adopt God's values and begin living toward God's ideals. Often, these changes occur quietly and slowly, but they happen for sure. A daughter who constantly hears her father affirm her preciousness develops a strong sense of self worth. What goes in comes out. As we get into the Word, it gets into us, and we are transformed by it. We become more like God. It molds us into an image of His Son, Jesus Christ. Thus, Scripture is usually our chief discipline for personal spiritual formation. Scripture has the power to change who we are, how we think, and how we live. Scripture changes us when it gets inside us. So, what are the ways we get Scripture inside us?

Devotional Reading

By far the most common means of absorbing Scripture is *devotional reading*—reading the Bible to hear what God has to say through it *to me*. Devotional reading of Scripture is more than reading a devotional book. It is reading *Scripture* devotionally. This kind of reading can be perilous, of course, for we could easily read our own desires into just about any verse. Yet through all of history, from the early Desert Fathers to today, believers have read the Bible this way. God has chosen to meet His people in the words of the Bible. God does indeed "speak" to us personally by using texts that meant something quite different when they were first written. Bible scholars tremble when ordinary Christians announce that God used a certain verse to tell them to accept a new job

> Then he opened their minds so they could understand the Scriptures.
>
> —Luke 24:45

they've been praying about. The Bible scholar mutters under her breath, "That verse is about the nation of Israel, not your new job—it was written to a group of people 2,500 years ago about their future, not to you personally about your career!" The ordinary Christian is unconvinced. They accept that the Bible had an "original meaning" and was written to an "original audience," yet they still believe God speaks to them personally about very different matters through those same words. This is devotional reading. It is using the Bible to hear a personal word from God. Could God take a verse that was originally directed to one rich man long ago and use that verse to tell St. Anthony to sell all and follow Jesus full time? Well, He did. Most Christians would agree that God does speak this way through the Bible. A devotional interpretation does not apply to all people at all times, but it can apply to one person here and now. When we read the Bible this way, we are really using it as a sort of prayer mechanism—a way to listen for God's voice *through* Scripture. It is the most popular way we use the Bible today. When we practice devotional reading, we are really listening to the Holy Spirit, who in turn uses the words of Scripture to speak to us. The Spirit could use a dictionary if He wanted to, but we are more likely to hear His prompting rightly through Scripture than from a dictionary. Devotional reading has its limitations and dangers, but it becomes far less dangerous if we also *study* the Scriptures.

And how from infancy you have known the holy Scriptures, which are able to make you wise for salvation through faith in Christ Jesus. All Scripture is God-breathed and is useful for teaching, rebuking, correcting and training in righteousness, so that the man of God may be thoroughly equipped for every good work.

—2 Timothy 3:15–17

Study

Bible study is a serious effort to discover what the Bible meant when it was written, and then to draw out what it means for us today.

Study takes us into the text to discover what the words meant to their original audience and how they would have been heard when the Bible was written. Once we've discovered what the verses meant when they were written, we then can move to *apply* that truth to today's world. Study can become a leash on our devotional interpretations of Scripture, reining them in and making them conform to meaning of the whole Bible. In study we often employ additional resources like study Bibles, commentaries, and books. Study takes us into the world of the Patriarchs, before there was a Bible or the Ten Commandments. It lets us visit ancient Israel and makes the Psalms spring alive before us. Study enables us to travel through time to the first century and see how women and children were treated in those days so that we can make sense of the Bible's instructions for women in worship. Today's church has a hundred devotional readers for every one person willing to seriously study the Scriptures. If we had more study of the Bible, we'd have less error in the church.

Memorization

There was a time when memorizing Scripture enjoyed the dominance that daily devotions do today. Many Christians now can't imagine that for the first 1,500 years of Christian history (and throughout the Old Testament period), printed Bibles were rare or unavailable. Until modern times the only Bible the average Christian had was what they heard read aloud on Sundays or had committed to memory. There were no Bibles sitting on end tables or stacked neatly in pew racks (there weren't even seats in churches for most of that time; people stood). For hundreds of years, most Christians didn't have the luxury of taking a break from cutting hay to read a few

> Whatever merit there is in anything that I have written is simply due to the fact that when I was a child my mother daily read me a part of the Bible and daily made me learn a part of it by heart.
>
> —John Ruskin

verses from their pocket New Testament. It is no wonder they went to church more often and memorized Scripture. It is a rare Christian today who makes a serious attempt to memorize Scripture, and we have lost something by abandoning that discipline. We no longer have Scripture on the tips of our tongues or in our heads. We no longer know where a verse is located—we say, "Somewhere in the Bible it says . . . " and then quote Benjamin Franklin's almanac and not Scripture. The greatest loss we suffer from our failure to memorize Scripture is the absence of a mental library of verses to meditate and ponder upon throughout the day. Memorizing Scripture builds our library a verse at a time. Then we can call it up, contemplate it, and apply it to life's situations as we face them. When we have few verses memorized, we will relegate Scripture to a few corners of life, such as morning devotions or church. When tempted in the wilderness, Jesus was able to quote specific scriptures related to each temptation. Memorizing Scripture prepares us to resist the devil. It changes us—that, of course, is what we really mean when we say that we've learned a Scripture "by heart."

> Do not merely listen to the word, and so deceive yourselves. Do what it says. Anyone who listens to the word but does not do what it says is like a man who looks at his face in a mirror and, after looking at himself, goes away and immediately forgets what he looks like. But the man who looks intently into the perfect law that gives freedom, and continues to do this, not forgetting what he has heard, but doing it—he will be blessed in what he does.
>
> —James 1:22–25

Meditation

Meditation is turning Scripture over in our minds, pondering it slowly. This is often done after we've memorized a passage, but it can be done as a means of reading Scripture as well. It is digesting the words slowly, ruminating on them, and reverentially allowing them to soak into our consciousness. This sort of reading is sometimes called *lectio divina* (divine reading), and is often seen as a means of finding union with God. When we meditate on Scripture, we let the words marinate in our minds and seep deeply into our hearts. As we do this, fresh truths emerge and clearer direction comes from God. We do not have to know much Scripture to begin meditating—almost all Christians already know The Lord's Prayer, John 3:16, and at least some of the Twenty-Third Psalm. With these few verses, we can begin the practice of meditation as we drive our car, take the elevator, or walk to and from the parking lot at work. While Eastern religions sometimes train their followers to meditate as a means of clearing the mind to arrive at complete emptiness, Christian meditation aims to fill the mind—with Scripture. As we do this, God's values gradually displace our own, and we start thinking more like God. This is the power of Scripture—from it, we gain the mind of God.

Hearing the Word

The Scriptures were not originally intended for silent reading. They were meant to be read aloud—to be *heard*. Today we engage Scripture with our eyes. Throughout most of Christian history, Scripture did not enter people's minds through their eyes but through their ears. This is why early church leaders were urged to give themselves to the "public reading" of Scripture—that's how people gained access to God's Word. In fact, most of the New Testament was not written to any individual; it was addressed to a group and was meant to be read to the entire gathered church. Hearing Scripture is different from seeing it. The ear detects different nuances in the Bible. Hearing Scripture

I meditate on your
  precepts
and consider your
  ways.
I delight in your
  decrees;
I will not neglect
  your word.

—Psalm 119:15–16

changes how we perceive it. We hear some Scripture readings at church—so long as we don't open the pew Bible and read along—but we can experience this transformational listening at home or in the car by means of sound recordings, or we can read the Bible aloud to ourselves and hear the shift in meaning as we listen to Scripture even in our own voice. When reading Scripture aloud, we automatically interpret it by our tones, inflections, and style of reading. Even if we listen to recorded scriptures and "zone out" after several chapters, the words still affect us even when we think we're not listening. Isn't that what we tell teenagers about their music? Sure, active listening is better. But even passive listening can change a person.

Doing the Word

Our objective is more than reading, study, memorizing, and meditating on the Word—it is *living* the word—that we are after. The Bible was not given for our information but for our transformation. To Protestants the Bible is almost a sacrament—a God-ordained place where He chooses to meet with and transform His people—a primary means of grace. When we come under its influence, Scripture makes us into something new and different and more like Christ. Perhaps the reason we are not enough like Christ is that too few of us make the Bible prominent in our lives. The spiritual discipline of Scripture gets us into the stream where God is moving so that we might be healed, becoming whole and transformed into the image of His Son, Jesus Christ.

How to Begin Practicing Scripture

Spread Your Bibles Out

How many Bibles do you own? Two? Five? Seven? Distribute them around the areas in which you live and work—one for the living room, another in the bedroom, one in the office by the computer, another in the car, and so on. There's no use piling them all up in one place. Make them accessible. Then watch how the Holy Spirit will prompt you to pick a Bible up and read it from time to time. Every person reading these words could do at least this.

Start Where You Are

What are you already doing with Scripture? List the ways in which you already practice this discipline, and don't be discouraged at how far short you fall from the ideal. You've got to start somewhere. For example, make a list of how many verses you already have memorized—the Lord's Prayer, perhaps, and some others—start with what you know.

Begin Having Daily Devotions

If you've been thinking about doing this for years but never started, this week would be a good time to begin. Or, more likely, you might have a sporadic practice of personal Bible reading and prayer, so this week would be a great time to begin *daily* devotions—even if you do it for only ten minutes at a time. Setting too high a devotional goal defeats many well-intentioned Christians. Set reachable goals that could reasonably be continued throughout your life, and don't increase them for months, maybe even years. The other disciplines in this book will take up some of your time also; there's more to do besides reading Scripture. Sure you could go "whole hog" with all these disciplines, but then you'd have no time for work, family, or even sleep. So start off carefully and go for consistency, not discipline-mania. Do something this week and do it *every day*. Start small.

Get a Scripture CD

If you were attracted to the notion of *listening* to the Scriptures, order or borrow one of the many inexpensive Scripture recordings that are available. If you especially enjoy music, consider buying a recording of scriptures sung or recorded with musical accompaniment. Put them in your car or near your CD player, and decide what sort of habit you'll create in order to listen regularly—like playing them every Sunday morning as you're getting ready for church or on Wednesdays during your commute to work. You'll love how this sooths and transforms your spirit—and it's easy too.

Journal Scripture

Simply start copying portions of Scripture in your own handwriting—slowly and thoughtfully, with reverence, as the scribes and monks once did. This may seem silly at first. After all, with modern printing presses and computer programs, you could just print out the verses, but stay with it. Watch what happens to you by the time you've done half of a book of the Bible. People who journal Scripture perhaps know best of all the transforming power of these words. Writing by hand slows down the usually rushed pace at which you consume Scripture and forces you to meditate on the words as you write. If you have an artistic flair, you may find yourself drawing doodles or other pictures alongside the text—exactly as many monks did in the past. If you've never done this, it may sound strange. But give it a try and see how transforming it will be for you—even when you copy familiar texts.

Set a Study Time

To avoid the trap of spending 100 percent of Bible time in devotional reading, set a time when you'll seriously study the Word. What would you set as a balanced schedule to blend both devotional reading and Bible study? A 100-percent-study type person needs to add more devotional reading. A 100-precent-devotional-reader needs to upgrade the amount of study. Most mature Christians would say a balanced approach to both devotional reading and study is best.

Start a Memorization Plan

With a partner, start a plan for memorizing Scripture so you can meditate on it. Be careful to avoid making this a race, as if the goal is simply to memorize a greater number of verses. Instead, measure your success at memory work by the number of verses you implement in your life. The memory goal is not learning but living.

Now What about You?

What are your specific plans to practice the discipline of Scripture this week?

Helps for leading your class or small group through this chapter are located at the back of this book.

Chapter 11

Charity

For I was hungry and you gave me something to eat, I was thirsty and you gave me something to drink, I was a stranger and you invited me in, I needed clothes and you clothed me, I was sick and you looked after me, I was in prison and you came to visit me.

Matthew 25:35

Charity is giving aid to the poor, motivated by a selfless love. It is love in action, love with gloves on, sometimes known as the biblical virtue of *lovingkindness*. While an organization dedicated to helping the poor may be called a charity, charity is a personal discipline as well. It is both central to the Christian faith and an evidence of it. This spiritual discipline is not merely an attitude of pity or a feeling of love but an action that helps. In the Bible, charity is referred to as almsgiving, and it was simply expected of the Israelites and of Jesus' disciples. James the brother of Jesus considered charity a test of pure religion, an evidence that we are indeed followers of God. This discipline changes the lives of both the poor and those who practice it. When we practice charity, we find fulfillment as God uses our hands do His work in the world. We take up Christ's work, becoming His hands, His feet, His gift to the poor.

God's Concern for the Poor

"God must especially love the poor because He made so many of them." The wisecrack is only half right. God does love the poor, but it is not God who made them poor. Why does He care so much about the poor? He cares because of who He is—He is a God of compassion. Christ illustrated this. He came to earth primarily as a savior not a healer, yet the Gospels report scores of healings. Why? Why didn't Jesus simply get on with "His father's business" of preaching the truth and dying for our sins? Jesus healed precisely because He *was* doing His father's business. Jesus inaugurated His earthly mission by proclaiming that His goal was to help the poor (Luke 4:18–19), and He named healing as an evidence of His true identity when questioned about it by John the Baptist (Luke 7:22). Christ showed His compassion for people in need. By doing so, He was showing us what God is like. Jesus Christ is God-in-action. God cares for the poor. So we might ask, "If He cares so much about the poor, why doesn't He send angels to help them?" The answer is that He has. He has sent us.

> Real charity doesn't care if it's tax-deductible or not.
>
> —Dan Bennett

> However, there should be no poor among you, for in the land the Lord your God is giving you to possess as your inheritance, he will richly bless you.
>
> —Deuteronomy 15:4

The Undeserving Poor

We who are well off sometimes wonder if the poor are victims of their own laziness and lack of motivation. We are tempted to think that the poor are poor because they don't have the gumption to scramble their way up the ladder as we have and as our parents did.

We think helping the poor might actually increase their reliance on handouts and complicate the search for a long-term solution. We are attracted to slogans like "God helps those who help themselves," which we have elevated to almost-scriptural status. (That saying, by the way, is from Aesop's fables, and goes "The gods help them that help themselves.") We worry that the poor may be undeserving and so our handout won't really help. We see poor people in the grocery store purchasing frivolous junk food and decide they aren't entitled to our help. We conclude that the poor are poor because they are lazy, ignorant, or stupid. Is that really our attitude? Do we really believe that grace should be given only to those who deserve it? If we think this way, we are ungodly. For God helps those who *don't* help themselves. Indeed, the essence of grace is giving to the undeserving. God gives to us in spite of the fact that we are unworthy. We should do the same for others. It is simply what Christians do.

> If your enemy is hungry, give him food to eat;
> if he is thirsty, give him water to drink.
>
> —Proverbs 25:21

Shutting Off Compassion

Concluding that the poor are undeserving causes us to shut up our "bowels of compassion" (as one version of the Bible puts it), which in turn shuts down our inclination toward lovingkindness. It is a kind of charity constipation. As our clenched-fist attitude toward the poor spreads, we gradually become a stingy person. Eventually, we withhold generosity from even our loved ones—for they, too, are undeserving. Charity is the antidote to this tight-fisted, stingy, lonely life. In the discipline of charity, we happily give to the poor whether they are deserving or undeserving. After all, the Bible

> And now abideth faith, hope, charity, these three; but the greatest of these is charity.
>
> —1 Corinthians 13:13 KJV

does not call us to help only the deserving needy. It simply commands us to give alms to the poor. In this we are called to be like God. He did not stoop to save us because we deserved it. He rescued us because He loved us. Our salvation by God is the ultimate act of charity, awarded to totally undeserving spiritual paupers—us! So when we help the poor—*especially* the undeserving ones—we are being like God. And we will gain as much from our act of charity as the poor do.

The Role of Government

Governments do more for the poor today than they did in Bible times. Yet even the ancient Israelites were required to give a "poor tithe" for the social programs of the day. They were also commanded to give alms personally, above this poor tithe. Admittedly, the situation is more complicated today. Some of our taxes do go to help the poor. That should be good news to us—we have a head start on almsgiving. But we need to finish the work we have begun. Perhaps we need to start thinking of a portion of our taxes as alms and thus pay them "as unto the Lord," meaning cheerfully. That might improve our attitude when taxes are due. However, few of us would say, "The government should do it all!" We recognize the need for charity above and beyond government programs, and individuals seem to do charity better than governments or groups do anyway. Few of us get the same satisfaction from paying taxes that we get from helping a person we know by name. Governments can provide a basic safety net for the poor, but we Christians can step in and provide the rest—along with meeting even deeper spiritual needs that no government can meet.

What good is it, my brothers, if a man claims to have faith but has no deeds? Can such faith save him? Suppose a brother or sister is without clothes and daily food. If one of you says to him, "Go, I wish you well; keep warm and well fed," but does nothing about his physical needs, what good is it?

—James 2:14–16

Defining Poverty

> If anyone has material possessions and sees his brother in need but has no pity on him, how can the love of God be in him? Dear children, let us not love with words or tongue but with actions and in truth.
>
> —1 John 3:17–18

How bad off do people have to be for us to consider them poor? Most of us are tempted to draw the poverty line so low that we'll seldom or never meet anyone whom we could really label *poor*. We see needy people around us and say, "There are millions of people around the world who would love to exchange places with them," thereby excusing ourselves from helping them. So whom should we help? The answer to that question is another question: whom did Jesus help? He helped those in need. He did not ask if they were frugal, if they deserved a handout, if they were reckless, or if they had sinned and caused their own sickness. He helped them because He had the resources and they had the need. He even helped the rich when He could. He did not say, "This military commander is far better off than I, why should I heal his son?" (see Matt. 8:5–13). He simply helped whomever He could because He was "very God" and that is what God does. We should too.

The Poor and Evangelism

> The angel answered, "Your prayers and gifts to the poor have come up as a memorial offering before God."
>
> —Acts 10:5

It is no coincidence that virtually every great evangelistic revival in history has been accompanied by a parallel revival in caring for the poor. A burden for lost souls and concern for the poor are twin passions; they feed on each other. Could it be that the lack of passion for souls that is so common in today's church is related to our lack of concern for the poor? If we were better at helping those with empty hearts, would we get better at helping those with empty shelves? Or visa versa? After all, both evangelism and charity spring from the same source—loving compassion.

Actively Seeking the Needy

> Charity sees the need, not the cause.
>
> —German proverb

How could we refuse a hungry person if we knew they were really hungry? No Christian would. Even people who aren't Christians help poor people when confronted with a need. Christians do not fail when they see needs up close; we just fail by arranging our lives so that we never see needy people. If we saw them, we would help them. Most of us can go weeks without seeing a poor person. We circulate in different orbits than they do. But Christians go find the needy. Just as we are commanded to find those in spiritual poverty and bring them riches in Christ, we are likewise commanded to find those in material poverty and bring them aid. Most people help those in need when they happen to see them. Christians go searching for needy people. We are evangelistic about both bodies and souls. We go to the "highways and byways," searching for needy people as described in the story of the great banquet in Luke 14. We don't just hang about our cozy homes and comfortable churches promising we'll help the poor if they show up. Most of them never will show up. Serious Christians get into life-saving boats and go to sea to rescue people in need, refusing to sit in our warm lighthouses waiting for the shipwrecked to wash up on shore. Christ came to seek and to save the lost. We Christians do the same.

> Religion that God our Father accepts as pure and faultless is this: to look after orphans and widows in their distress and to keep oneself from being polluted by the world.
>
> —James 1:27

Giving Our Time

It may be harder to give our time than our money. For some of us, money is more plentiful than time. Charitable organizations are desperate for volunteers. When we volunteer our time, more aid gets to the poor because the organization does not have to hire somebody to do the work. Another advantage of giving time over money is that it increases the change in our hearts. Who finds the same satisfaction in writing a check as in serving a meal to a needy person? The Good Samaritan probably found greater joy in helping the beaten traveler face to face than he had found in paying that year's poor tithe. Those of us who call ourselves Christians might consider giving our time along with our money. We'd be happier people if we did. That is not to say that the poor are always grateful. Sometimes they're abusive and do not express the sort of thanks we think they should. We don't either, when it comes to God's grace given to us. Perhaps for that reason alone we ought to help the ungrateful poor—it is like looking in the mirror.

"You will always have the poor among you, but you will not always have me."

—John 12:8

The Invisible Poor

The trouble with Charles Dickens's notion that "charity begins at home" is that most of us don't get far enough away from home to see the needy people who don't happen to live nearby. But God loves them too. While beginning our charity at home seems like a nice notion, charity shouldn't begin *and end* at home. Our commission is global, not local. The greatest poverty in our world is found across oceans in out-of-the-way places we will never visit. The plight of the world's poor breaks God's heart, and He

A bone to the dog is not charity. Charity is the bone shared with the dog, when you are just as hungry as the dog.

—Jack London

> Now this was the sin of your sister Sodom: She and her daughters were arrogant, overfed and unconcerned; they did not help the poor and needy.
>
> —Ezekiel 16:49

expects us to do something about it. Millions of people die from starvation every year. We see glimpses of them on television. Today, some forty thousand children will die from malnutrition and disease. Certainly these souls deserve our attention, don't they? The Bible says that God "so loved *the world*." While we quibble about welfare benefits for the poor in our own nations, millions more starve to death far from our homes. They do not want a shirt or pair of pants—they want something to eat so they can survive one more day. At times entire countries become death camps due to famine. They are full of gaunt, emaciated ghostlike people who lack enough food to reach tomorrow. These needy people lay broken and bleeding by the global roadside, too weak to call for our help. They are largely out of our sight. What shall we do? What would Jesus do? What did the Good Samaritan do? The answer is obvious. We Christians will send whatever aid we can. It is the Christly thing to do. What else could we do? Go golfing to forget these people?

Spiritual Gains

Charity is a good work, but what makes it a *spiritual* discipline? The answer is simple: taking up the discipline of charity brings us closer to God. As we do His work, we find ourselves beside Him. God is already with the poor. And when we show up, we find Him near. We will one day face Him, and He will remind us of the treatment we gave Him. *Him*? Yes, when we help the needy, we are judged by Christ to have fed, clothed, visited and cared for Christ himself

> I never add up. I only subtract from the total dying. . . . It is not the magnitude of our actions but the amount of love that is put into them that matters.
>
> —Mother Teresa

(Matt. 25). And the poor themselves will sometimes inspire our faith. We will develop new levels of gratitude and sense God's blessing on our labor. We will often see among the poor greater generosity than we see among our friends. Even if we cure nothing at all and fail to change the world one bit, *we* will be changed. For charity is a means of grace. As we make the world a better place, God makes us better persons. For it is in giving that we receive.

How to Begin Practicing Charity

Celebrate What You Are Already Doing

First, assess what you are already doing. Many Christians are more involved with the poor than they realize. Take an honest assessment of what you are doing personally and what your family and church are doing to help the poor. Find out what percentage of your taxes goes to poor people and celebrate it. Don't let this chapter make you feel like a bad Christian. Instead, let it inspire you to be a better one. Start by celebrating what you already are doing.

Plan a Drive-Through

If you feel distant from the poor in your community, plan a Sunday afternoon drive—not in the country, but through the area of your town where needy people live. Drive slowly and let God lay a burden on your heart. If you can, stop and visit people—not to "help" yet, but just to learn and feel and to make friends.

Begin Even if You Don't Feel Compassion

Even if you feel no compassion for the poor, start doing something to help them. After all, that's why we call it a spiritual *discipline*—it takes determination. You can help the poor without feeling compassion, but you cannot do it for long. Seeing poverty face to face has a way of bringing out Christ's compassion that is deep in our hearts.

Start a Food Pantry

A food pantry won't solve the world's hunger problem, but it is a start. Face it, nothing you do will solve the world's poverty problem. Nor will anything you do solve the world's sin problem. But we should do what we can anyway. It is in trying that we obey God's commands. So start with a simple act like organizing a food pantry at your church or even for your Sunday school class or small group.

Start Volunteering Your Time This Week

If you were to become an active volunteer serving poor people, to what organization would you contribute your time? What is your favorite charitable organization? Why not start this week by taking the first step—call to offer your time.

Sign Up for a Missions Trip

Sign up for a trip where you will see abject poverty that will haunt you for the rest of your life. See poverty as God sees it—up close and personal. You will be permanently altered if you do this. So will everyone you live with. It may be better to spend your money on this trip than to give it to your poor nephew struggling to pay his college tuition. When you have seen the world as God sees it, you will never again be "normal."

Take an Offering for the Poor

In some churches any nondesignated offering received on the first Sunday of each month goes to almsgiving. When might your church take an offering to help the poor, as Christ expects us to do? Or when could your class do it? Or, if nobody else seems excited at the prospect, when could you take an offering from yourself and see that it helps the poor?

Adopt a New Lifestyle

This book only asks you to try a spiritual discipline for one week then move on to another. Yet some of these disciplines would make good lifelong habits. Most Christians will practice prayer or Bible reading the rest of their lives. Few will do that with this discipline. Is God calling you to take up this discipline in a more serious way, representing the rest who will pass it by and forget it by next month?

Now What about You?

What are your specific plans to practice charity this week?

Helps for leading your class or small group through this chapter are located at the back of this book.

Chapter 12

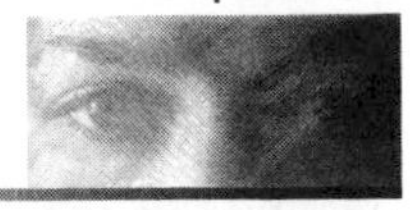

Prayer

In the same way, the Spirit helps us in our weakness. We do not know what we ought to pray for, but the Spirit himself intercedes for us with groans that words cannot express.

Romans 8:26

Prayer is a conversation with God through which we come to know Him better and develop greater reliance on Him. Prayer is not just asking God for things. It is less about getting things than about getting things right. Prayer is a means of drawing near to God and sensing Him draw near to us. In prayer we pledge allegiance to God and assert our total reliance on His grace. It is perhaps the oldest spiritual discipline, preceding Scripture by several thousand years. Prayer may be the most fundamental spiritual discipline.

An Intangible Discipline

While we know prayer is important, most of us in the Western world don't practice prayer very well. We're too task oriented. We want to get something done, check something off our to-do list, and make some progress. Maybe this is why we prefer Bible reading to prayer. We can count the chapters we've read or verses we've memorized and see measurable "progress." Prayer, however, is so . . . *spiritual*. And we are more a practical people than a spiritual people.

Bless those who curse you, pray for those who mistreat you.

—Luke 6:28

The Value of Prayer

Some of us find it hard to pray because we are not sure it does any good. If we see God as a distant First Cause who set the laws of the universe in motion but seldom steps in and breaks those laws, we'll find it hard to pray. Many favor this God-concept and are thus slow to make any special requests of Him. Others see God as an all-wise and all-loving person who will always provide exactly what we need, so we think, "Who are we to tell God what to do?" We don't want to pester God with our requests, and we're sure we don't know how to give Him advice. So we simply trust God instead of praying to Him. And it may be that some of us seldom pray because we think prayer is useless. We see God as Absolute Sovereign of the universe who has predetermined every event that will ever take place. We believe that nothing humans can do will ever change God's mind or affect His behavior. Why pray if God has already decided what He will do anyway? However, most of us do not pray enough simply because we are too busy. We are too busy to hear the Spirit's reminders to pray. So for whatever reason, there is a general prayerlessness among many Christians in the Western world, not counting the momentary prayers we make throughout the day or at mealtimes. We may be

The Spirit, when He prays through us, or helps us to meet the mighty "oughtness" of right praying, trims our praying down to the will of God.

—R. A. Torrey

passable in our practice of Bible reading and do all right at writing prayer letters, designing prayer chains, holding prayer conferences, making prayer requests, and writing and reading chapters on prayer. It is just the actual praying that we do poorly.

Reasons to Pray

> Work, work, from morning until late at night. In fact, I have so much to do that I shall have to spend the first three hours in prayer.
>
> —Martin Luther

Many of us fail to pray because we do not understand the nature of prayer. We assume the primary purpose for prayer is to ask God for things, so we have many excuses to skip praying and "simply trust Him." But prayer is much more than asking God for things. Prayer is more than petition. In prayer we also praise God for His goodness, confess our sins, express gratitude, confirm our faith, and draw closer to God. Prayer, at its core, is not about asking for things but about cultivating a relationship between God and us. Prayer is about communion, fellowship, and even union with God. Prayer is not merely a way to manipulate some divine vending machine in order to get what we want, a divine lottery in which lucky people occasionally hit the right number. Prayer is not a way to use God but a way to offer ourselves to be used by Him. Prayer binds us to God so that we gain His perspective. It does not change His mind so much as it changes *our* minds—and *our* hearts. After being with God, we see the glaring disparity between His values and the world's ideals, the church's values and even our own standards. Prayer changes our hearts, our minds, and our desires so that we begin to feel God's emotions, think God's thoughts, and want God's will. Prayer is not just about changing life; it's about changing *us*. In short, prayer is a means of sanctifying us, of spiritually

> And Satan trembles when he sees
> The weakest saint upon his knees.
>
> —William Cowper

forming us into an image of God's own Son. Yet there is another reason to pray. Prayer is a powerful personal statement of faith. It is mighty hard to pray without believing in God. By praying, we proclaim that we indeed believe in God. Prayer is our personal statement of faith, our pledge of allegiance to God. An anemic prayer life illustrates a feeble faith—how can we assert there is a God if we don't talk to Him? Prayer is the voice of faith.

Prayer lays hold of God's plan and becomes the link between His will and its accomplishment on earth. Amazing things happen, and we are given the privilege of being the channels of the Holy Spirit's prayer.

—Elisabeth Elliot

How to Pray

So how should we pray? Jesus' disciples asked the same question. We don't know exactly what they thought of His answer. We do know that most evangelicals don't think much of it. Jesus replied to their question by giving them a prayer to pray—we call it the Lord's Prayer. Most of us don't like to repeat a fixed prayer. We like variety and think we can pray in our own words better than using the words Jesus taught us to pray. So we pretend that Scripture means, "Pray after this pattern." We would not fit in with the early Christians, who took Christ's words to mean exactly what they say. Those Christians prayed the Lord's Prayer itself. In fact, they prayed it three times a day, every single day. But most evangelicals, in fleeing "formal religion," have abandoned praying the prayer Christ taught and thus do not take His teaching literally, on this point anyway. Perhaps we are right—maybe the Lord's Prayer was intended only as a model, and the early Christians got it wrong. But before we discard

Do not be anxious about anything, but in everything, by prayer and petition, with thanksgiving, present your requests to God.

Philippians 4:6

the prayer itself, we should remember that the early church prayed this prayer daily in worship and that the vast majority of Christians have prayed this exact prayer for two thousand years. So perhaps we might pray it at least occasionally. Some Christians pray the Lord's Prayer before each meal. It is an error to take the Lord 's Prayer lightly. Some do that by praying it too much—with such ritual blandness that they forget its meaning. Others take it lightly by praying it too little—with such abandonment of ritual that they also forget its meaning. Mainline Christians may make the first error, but evangelicals certainly are guilty of the second.

> Any concern too small to be made into a prayer is too small to be made into a burden.
>
> —Corrie Ten Boom

What to Pray About

If we did determine that the Lord's Prayer is an outline for praying, what does it teach us about prayer? The prayer begins by teaching us the relationship that we have in prayer—that of a child to a loving *Father*. The prayer then immediately redirects our mind from earthly things to God's abode, *heaven*. We are taught adoration as we *hallow* God's name. This initial focus on God and heaven aligns our values with God's so that when we return to earthly matters, we pray about God's concerns first—God's *kingdom* coming *on earth* so that His *will is done* here on earth the way it is in heaven. Then we pray for personal needs. We ask for *daily bread*—the essentials needed to sustain life—but then quickly shift to asking *forgiveness* for our sins, implying that we will also forgive others. Speaking of sin, we are taught to plead for escape from *temptation* and deliverance *from evil*. Then Protestants close with a final doxology of praise that was added sometime after Jesus taught the prayer, acknowledging that to God belong the *kingdom, power, and glory forever*.

> But Jesus often withdrew to lonely places and prayed.
>
> —Luke 5:16

> Then he said to them, "Suppose one of you has a friend, and he goes to him at midnight and says, 'Friend, lend me three loaves of bread, because a friend of mine on a journey has come to me, and I have nothing to set before him.'
> "Then the one inside answers, 'Don't bother me. The door is already locked, and my children are with me in bed. I can't get up and give you anything.' I tell you, though he will not get up and give him the bread because he is his friend, yet because of the man's boldness he will get up and give him as much as he needs.
>
> —Luke 11:5–8

What a glimpse into God's prayer list! Perhaps we improve on Christ's original words in our casual, ad lib prayers, but we will not improve on His content. Christ taught us to praise God, pray about His kingdom, our necessities, forgiveness, temptation, and deliverance from evil. Even if we use the Lord's Prayer as a model prayer and not an actual prayer to be prayed, most Christians will have to adjust their prayer outline—to the things Jesus taught us to pray about. This will mean more prayer for the kingdom of God and spiritual matters like temptation and sin and less prayer about our own requests and the guidance we want to receive from God. Throughout history, those who have thought they could improve on the original instructions of Christ have faded away. The Lord's Prayer always makes a comeback.

It's-All-about-Me Prayer

Sometimes our extemporaneous prayers get off balance because they come from inside us. We will always pray too much about ourselves if left to ourselves. Unplanned prayers have more passion but sometimes are merely mirrors of our own desires and preoccupations. For most of us, our insides are full of, well, *us*. Too many of us are self-centered folk, intent on bettering our lives. We use prayer as a means to improve our situation, get guidance about decisions, feel better equipped for the day, and gain insight on how to manage our relationships with others. These are not wrong uses of prayer, but they usually dominate our prayer life. And that shows us to be out of balance in light of the concerns in the Lord's Prayer. In order to resist the temptation to make self-centered prayers, Christians often use the Lord's Prayer as outline. By sticking to its agenda, they monitor the balance of their prayers. Others use the familiar ACTS rubric (Adoration, Confession, Thanksgiving, and Supplication) to do the same. By whatever means, most of us need to find a way to become less self-centered and more Kingdom-centered in our praying.

> It is possible to move men, through God, by prayer alone.
>
> —Hudson Taylor

Adoration

Great "prayer warriors" almost always begin their prayers with *adoration,* giving God glory and praise for who He is. Adoration is not thanking God—it is adoring Him for His essence, His character. It is not that God has poor self-esteem and needs to be cheered up. God does not need our sweet talk. We need to confess God's greatness so we are reminded of it ourselves. This is what bonds us to Him and brings us near. Adoration makes *this* God *our* God. In adoration we recite the qualities of God's character, and that reminds us of what we want to become. Adoration is worship. Few of us are in danger of giving God too much adoration in our prayers. Our error is making too many petitions. If we learned how to adore God better in prayer, we'd become better prayers. But to improve our adoration abilities would require study and preparation. If wc simply "pray from our heart," with no thought or training, what comes out is our inner stream of consciousness, which is usually preoccupied with ourselves and our daily concerns. God cares about our concerns, but He also wants us to care about His. In prayer we ought to capture what preoccupies the heart

> If you believe, you will receive whatever you ask for in prayer.
>
> —Matthew 21:22

> To get nations back on their feet, we must first get down on our knees.
>
> —Billy Graham

of God, not just fill the air with our own preoccupations. By doing some homework on the traits of God, we learn what it is about Him we should adore, and we can upgrade this part of our praying to include adoration. Bible study (especially of the Psalms) helps us know the character of God so that we won't rapidly skip over adoration or substitute thanksgiving, mislabeling it as praise. Adoration makes known the character of God.

Confession

In confession we admit our sins to God and ourselves. Confession is "coming clean" before God. If we confess our sins, He is faithful and will forgive us. Unconfessed sin is a barrier to our relationship with God, blocking us from drawing near. When we bring it all out into the light, we clear away that obstruction. Being honest with God ends our pretence that there is nothing wrong between God and us. Confession is admitting to God that "I am what I am" and that without Him, I'd be even worse. Refusing to tell God our hidden thoughts, feelings, attitudes, and desires keeps no secrets from God. Pretending to hide our true selves from God only perpetuates a false notion in our own minds—and no relationship can move far when one of the persons isn't honest. But there are things to confess besides sin. We confess our weaknesses and tendencies so that these, too, are brought into the light. We even confess our temptations. We acknowledge our own frailty and total dependence on God. When we confess, we see ourselves as we really are and become more dependent on God's grace. True and open confession introduces us to ourselves—we see ourselves as God sees us.

> Prayer is the exercise of drawing on the grace of God.
>
> —Oswald Chambers

Thanksgiving

In thanksgiving we recite God's "mighty acts," expressing gratitude for what He has done throughout history and in our own lives. We do not do this because God forgets what He has done and needs reminding—we do it because *we* forget. We thank God for calling Abraham, for bringing the children of Israel through the Red Sea, for establishing the nation of Israel and raising up King David. We thank God for the calling the prophets and blessing and punishing the various kings. We thank Him for sending His Son, Jesus, and we thank Him for what Jesus did to heal the sick, raise the dead, and preach liberty. We thank God for raising Jesus from the dead, for establishing the church, for inspiring Christians to write the books of the New Testament, and for leading the church to select the right books for our Bible over the course of several hundred years. We thank God for His work around the world today and for all who serve Him. We thank God for how He is working in other churches and denominations. Finally, after thanking God for several thousand years' worth of graciousness, we are ready to turn to the present and our own lives. We thank Him for our own parents and family and for His provision and providence for loved ones and ourselves. We recite in detail His mighty acts done specifically for us. We thank Him for good things and bad things—for they both help us become more like Christ. Only after such a recitation of thanksgiving are we ready to ask God for anything.

One of those days Jesus went out to a mountainside to pray, and spent the night praying to God.

—Luke 6:12

And when you stand praying, if you hold anything against anyone, forgive him, so that your Father in heaven may forgive you your sins.

—Mark 11:25

Supplication

Supplication is asking God for something. This sort of praying is also called *petition*, or sometimes *intercession* when asking God on behalf of others. Many Christians merely tip their hat to adoration, confession, and thanksgiving, then rush into what they consider *real* praying—supplication. They are wrong in doing so. Yet after the proper preparation, we are instructed to ask God for things. All Christians are not good at asking God for things. Some Christians—and this seems even truer of men—are slow to make their requests known to God. Particularly for Americans, whose national values encourage self-reliance and personal responsibility more than dependence and submission, supplication is difficult. We are taught to be ashamed of being dependent or needy, except for short periods of time while we're trying to "get back on our feet." We think people ought to "stand on their own two feet" and "pull themselves up by their bootstraps." These values diminish our desire to pray. However, when it comes to our relationship with God, we have neither a foot to stand on nor bootstraps to pull on. We are totally helpless and utterly reliant on Him. So we make our requests known to Him. We even ask for things we think we'd get without asking—training ourselves to be thankful when any good thing comes our way. In supplication we make our desires known to God. Sometimes we desire things that really aren't good for us, and God purifies our desires during

> So I say to you: Ask and it will be given to you; seek and you will find; knock and the door will be opened to you. For everyone who asks receives; he who seeks finds; and to him who knocks, the door will be opened. Which of you fathers, if your son asks for a fish, will give him a snake instead? Or if he asks for an egg, will give him a scorpion? If you then, though you are evil, know how to give good gifts to your children, how much more will your Father in heaven give the Holy Spirit to those who ask him!
>
> —Luke 11:9–12

prayer so that while we first asked amiss, we later ask rightly. God does indeed answer prayer. God can be moved by His children's prayers, thus we have a part in the outcome of things. Life has not been rigged since the beginning of time so that we have no hope of influencing what God will do. We can affect the outcome of events through prayer. So we come boldly before God's throne, asking our Father the King to grant our requests. We are bold, yet not presumptuous—for we know that Jesus Christ, the model prayer, ended His own desperate prayer in the Garden of Gethsemane with the words "not my will, but thine, be done."

God shapes the world by prayer. The more praying there is in the world the better the world will be, the mightier the forces against evil.

—E. M. Bounds

Listening

Prayer is a conversation. A good conversation shouldn't be one sided. Prayer ought to be a two-way affair and not a one-sided monologue. God is a good listener, but He also has some things to say. It is poor manners to do all the talking. Prayer is a dialogue, not a filibuster. People who are good at prayer often just shut up and listen. Some of us like talking too much. We like hearing ourselves talk, and our prayers are not about God and His concerns but about us and our concerns. For us, prayer is a chance to talk to ourselves while God sits in the audience. Talkative types might need to discipline themselves to start *listening* for God's side of the conversation in prayer. He will speak—if we'll let Him get a word in edgewise.

How to Begin Practicing Prayer

Start a Daily Prayer Time

Pick a time each day this week for daily prayer. Stick to the schedule for an entire week.

Set a Time for Extended Prayer

Pick at least one longer time period this week in which you will do nothing but pray. Don't check anything off your list, and allow no way to measure your "progress" by reading or writing. Practice the pure *spiritual* discipline of prayer.

Pray the Scriptures

If you feel tongue-tied when you pray, simply look up the great prayers of the Bible and pray them. They were good enough to be written down for us, so why not use them? Simply turn to the Psalms or Epistles and seek out the prayers that best fit your needs, then pray them fervently.

Make a Prayer Outline

Are your prayers balanced? A prayer outline helps us police our prayers to make sure we give appropriate weight to items we might rush past to get to our favorite, more self-centered, parts. What would you include in your own prayer outline? What are the categories you ought to cover in prayer? In what order? Turn your answers into an outline you can follow in prayer.

Journal Your Prayers

Written prayers do not have to be stale and repetitive. They can be more meaningful, more thoughtful, and more powerful in their effect on you. If you enjoy writing, carefully write down your prayers, then use them to pray fervently.

Start a Prayer List

What are you praying for specifically? Do you keep a record of the answers to prayer you receive? Make a list of the requests you want to bring regularly to God. However, when making the list, integrate it to a full outline so you won't be trapped into thinking prayer is mostly petition. Include the other elements of balanced prayer on your prayer list as well.

Daily Pray the Lord's Prayer

Just in case the early Christians were right about this habit, try it for a week. Where could you fit the Lord 's Prayer into your life three times each day—usually tied to another habitual act? On arising? At bedtime? At mealtimes? Every time you get in your automobile? Think of three occasions during the course of a day when you could pray this prayer deliberately and carefully.

Pray in the Middle of the Night

Do you ever awaken at night and can't get back to sleep for awhile? Pray during these periods, every time. Instead of counting sheep, talk to the Shepherd.

Plan a Prayer Retreat

If you are taking the discipline of prayer very seriously, how about making plans for a prayer retreat, during which you would devote an entire day—perhaps even several days—entirely to prayer? Picking the date is the first step to making this happen.

Now What about You?

What are your specific plans to practice prayer this week?

Helps for leading your class or small group through this chapter are located at the back of this book.

Chapter 13

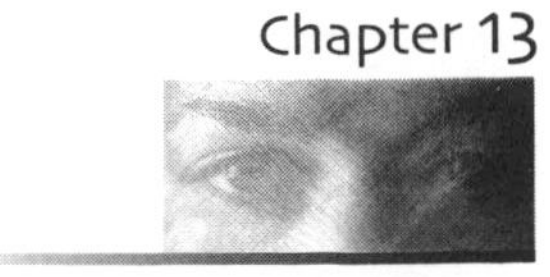

Penance

The Lord disciplines those he loves, and he punishes everyone he accepts as a son. Endure hardship as discipline; God is treating you as sons. For what son is not disciplined by his father? If you are not disciplined (and everyone undergoes discipline), then you are illegitimate children and not true sons.

Hebrews 12:6–8

Penance is willfully embracing earthly punishment for wrongdoing that has already been forgiven by God. It is done to rectify past wrongs and to make us better persons. Penance brings us into reconciliation with others and ourselves. Penance is the spiritual discipline of "doing our time" for what we have done wrong and of "making things right." In this discipline we do not try to earn God's forgiveness, but we assign consequences to ourselves for our wrongdoing. When we've wronged another person, penance voluntarily "makes it up to them" by balancing the earthly books. Penance is a means of disciplining and training ourselves.

The Reason for Penance

Most Protestants shun the notion of penance. We think it's "too Catholic," or that it's a way of earning God's forgiveness. Protestants believe there is nothing we can do to earn favor from God. Thus, penance smacks of "salvation by works" to us. But that is a grave misunderstanding of this discipline. Penance is for Protestants and Catholics alike—it is a *Christian* discipline. God's grace is indeed free of charge and comes through faith, not by human effort. But penance is not about bettering our relationship with God or earning forgiveness for sins. It is primarily about our relationship with others—and with ourselves. It is we who need to shed the burden of past wrongs that we still carry—burdens God has already forgiven! The spiritual discipline of penance often helps free us of these self-imposed burdens of guilt. And it trains us to avoid committing the same wrongs in the future.

Forgiveness and Consequences

If God doesn't need our penance, then who does? Others do. And we do. Being forgiven by God does not automatically make things right with the people we've wronged. Consider the case of a captivating pastor who is caught in a motel room with one of his parishioners. How quickly can God forgive this pastor? In a second. At the moment of true repentance, his slate will be cleared and the debt totally forgiven by God. But while God can forgive in an instant, humans naturally take longer. The church people whom this pastor deceived, along with his wife, will take longer to be reconciled to him than God will. Most church members think such a pastor should stop preaching. They would say he shouldn't "act as if nothing happened" or keep right on pastoring that church. And consider the

> We can never direct our penance to God. For we could never say to Him, "I'll make it up to you."
>
> —Beau Hummel

> So the Lord God banished him from the Garden of Eden to work the ground from which he had been taken.
>
> —Genesis 3:23

case of a criminal found guilty of murder who becomes a Christian while serving a life sentence in prison. Should he go free because he has been fully forgiven by God? Many Christians would say the murderer should still "do the time" or "pay his debt to society" even though his slate has been cleared with God. Most of us assume that people still have to face the temporal consequences for their wrongdoing even though they have escaped the eternal penalty. If we think this way, we have gotten the core idea of the spiritual discipline of penance. It is taking on earthly punishment for wrongdoing as a means of grace—a channel through which God makes us better people and brings us into reconciliation with others. In penance we *willingly* take on punishment as a means of making things right and training us for the future. Penance is the discipline of "paying our debt" to others even though our debt to God has been paid in full. Penance and restitution are so similar they are hard to differentiate—indeed if we don't like the term *penance*, we might substitute *restitution* and arrive at the same place. Restitution generally requires another party with whom to be reconciled. Penance is sometimes general in nature and related more to ourselves than to the people we have offended. Also, penance can relate to *groups* we have wronged. Zacchaeus may have practiced both kinds of penance. He promised direct restitution to individuals he had swindled, and he also promised to commit half of his wealth to the poor. The first act is what we often call restitution, the second penance.

'Little' Sins

Most of us would agree that there should be penance for things like murder. In fact, the term *penitentiary*, now merely a synonym for *prison*, has its root in the idea of penance. And most of us agree that

After Nathan had gone home, the Lord struck the child that Uriah's wife had borne to David, and he became ill. David pleaded with God for the child. He fasted and went into his house and spent the nights lying on the ground. The elders of his household stood beside him to get him up from the ground, but he refused, and he would not eat any food with them.

—2 Samuel 12:15–17

a mere "I'm sorry" responded to with "no problem" is not an adequate way of dealing with the adulterous pastor mentioned above. We can understand the need for penance after such "big" sins as these. But we balk at doing penance for wrongs we ourselves are guilty of—what we have labeled "little" sins. Yet it is our personal, seemingly minor, offenses that penance is precisely designed to remedy. Penance is a means of grace. Used rightly, it is a channel through which God changes us, helps us grow, and enables us to overcome sin and our wayward temperaments. It helps us stop doing wrong. It forms us into the image of Christ. When we take on the discipline of penance, we assign ourselves penalties for our wrongs in order to improve our behavior. These penalties do not earn forgiveness from God any more than our children's punishment earns our forgiveness. Penance is our training for the future. We use penance when we've spent an hour in a committee meeting and leave realizing we made several harsh and cutting remarks to one particular person. Penance is for people who recall how badly they treated a girl back in high school but realize it would not be wise to contact her now. Penance is for dads who promised their daughters to attend "every single soccer game this year" but just missed her second game. Penance is for the wife who realizes she has been ill-tempered all evening. Penance is for the employer who now admits he paid his workers less than they deserved for many years. Penance is for the person who used to toss trash out the car window when driving at night. It is for the middle-aged woman who remembers how cruelly she treated her now-deceased mother years ago. In short, penance is for everyone except perfect people. It is for all sins, even "little" sins, past and present wrongs, offenses committed by us personally and as a group.

Family Discipline

Parents intuitively understand penance. In an act of rage, a younger brother destroys his sister's science project the night before it is due. What do the parents do? They try to get the brother to repent. They demand he say "I'm sorry" to his sister. But is that all? Not for most parents. There will be *consequences* for his wrongdoing. Thus, children are sometimes spanked, sent to their rooms, grounded, sent to stand the corner, or excluded socially by getting "time out" to ponder their misdeeds. Do these punishments mean the parent has not forgiven the child? Not at all! Parents simply don't want to let their children off the hook with a quick "I'm sorry." They fear the children might assume they can do anything they please if they merely say "I'm sorry" afterward. So most parents take some action to discipline their children—to teach and train them away from anarchy and toward civilization. Penance brings this training to grownups too.

Three Steps after Wrongdoing

The first thing to do when we sin is to get forgiveness from God. This is the easier part, which is why it is the only part done by many Christians. Figuring God's forgiveness is all we need, we merrily go on our way, presuming the slate is clear. But it is not. Our wrong actions hurt others too. So the second step is going to the people we've wronged and asking for their forgiveness. This is much harder than asking God for forgiveness. How we hate to say, "I was wrong." But we must to

> It's most handy to organize sins in only two categories: major sins or minor sins, the former of which are done by others, the latter by myself.
>
> —John Leonard

bring reconciliation. How blessed are those who take the second step to gain forgiveness from people they've wronged! But there is a third step—penance. Most Christians understand the idea of penance when applied to stealing, for example. "Simply pay it back," we say. Or perhaps we'd say, "Pay it back with interest." Indeed, Jesus considered Zacchaeus's penance as clear evidence that he had indeed been changed. But the hard sort of penance is not financial but relational—righting the books with the *people* I've wronged. We might be willing to ask forgiveness, but should we then walk away "free and clear"? Human life does not work that way. If we've been secretly working for several years at destroying a coworker's reputation, asking their forgiveness is not enough. There is damage to repair. If we took up the discipline of penance, we'd set about an intentional campaign to reverse the effects of our undermining over the years. That could take years, as opposed to tossing a mere "I'm sorry" to the violated person. Getting forgiveness from God is easy and quick. Getting forgiveness from others is tricky and slow. Doing penance is the hardest and slowest of all. That is why this discipline is so rarely practiced. But penance is powerful in making us more like Christ. So it is hard, but it is worth it.

> God has forgiven him. Why can't we?
>
> —Parishioner arguing to retain a pastor who had committed adultery

Penance as Training

Penance is training. It provides the discipline to break bad habits and start good ones. Breaking a habit sometimes takes a bit of pain. In one company, the executives all wore a rubber band on their wrists, and they agreed to snap it hard any time they said the words *impossible* or *can't*. What began as a light-hearted stunt completely changed the atmosphere of the company. Self-imposed penance is like snapping that rubber band. It is "snapping" ourselves for our wrongs in order to train ourselves to do right.

Quiet Penance

> We detest taking on the discipline of penance because we hate to be reminded of our sins—which is precisely why we should take it up.
>
> —Garnet May Anderson

Penance is best done in secret. We have done wrong, and we know it. We feel compelled to balance the books and pay our debt, so we take on this discipline. But we ought to do it quietly. Indeed, penance does not always have to be related to the offense or the people who were wronged in order to be successful. We could decide that for the rest of our lives, we'll pick up trash every time we walk for exercise—not as a "good deed" but as an act of penance. We could determine to always return our shopping basket plus one other basket every time we go grocery shopping to remind us of the past wrongs we've done and to humble us. Or, our acts of penance might be directly related to our offenses. If we seldom visited our aged father in his final years, we might determine to go to a nursing home on the first Sunday afternoon of each month to visit people we don't yet know. Would we get benefit from this ministry? Certainly we would. But reminding ourselves each month of our unkindness in the past might train us to be more kind in the present and future. These are the sorts of things we do as the spiritual discipline of penance.

Inner Peace

Penance brings inner peace. God forgives us in a moment, and others may come to forgive us in time. But the hardest forgiveness to gain is from ourselves. We may be forgiven for that deed we did long ago yet still feel guilty. Even after the person we wronged hugs us and tells us it is all forgotten, we continue to feel guilty. Why? Often it is because we have not forgiven ourselves. The wealthy oil magnate who swindled his rancher brother out of the family ranch still feels guilty, even though he went forward at the Billy Graham rally

> I'll never listen to her music again—never in my whole life.
>
> —Former fan of a Christian musician who fell morally

in Dallas. What is wrong? His brother is dead and gone, but the rich man still feels guilty. The accusing finger he senses is his own. This man should take up the discipline of penance. He should begin to "pay off his debt" even if his brother has no heirs. The more he "makes things right," the less he will feel guilty. God forgave him freely and without cost. But he also knows in his heart that to keep the books right on earth somehow requires "paying his debt to society." He can do it with money or he can do it through serving others. What will make his actions a means of grace is his willingness to take on the discipline while believing that it is just that—a means God is using to make him a better person. He will come to know joy and freedom after doing penance. It will make him smile and chuckle to himself. He will feel frce again—as he did when he was a boy on the ranch. He will be released from the death grip of his self-inflicted guilt. In the discipline of penance, he will come to find the hardest forgiveness of all—forgiveness from himself.

The Danger of Penance

We must close this chapter as we began it: by reminding ourselves that this discipline can be a dangerous one. When we take on this spiritual discipline, it will be easy to let our minds slip into thinking that penance is something between God and us. If we do, it will become one more baby step on the path toward imagining that God is impressed with our good deeds and is piling them on the scales to outweigh the bad things we've done, finally tipping the balance toward heaven. This is false. Penance is not about God and us. It is about the relationship between others and us and between us and ourselves. In penance we pay off horizontal debt (to others), not our vertical debt (to God). And we find inner peace and personal satisfaction as we come to feel fully forgiven by others and ourselves.

How to Begin Practicing Penance

Ponder Past Wrongs

Begin by setting aside some time for pondering what deeds you would do penance for. Have you been perfect all your life, or are there some things you've done that are forgiven by God but are still "out of balance" with others? Take time to ponder what that might be. Don't get into a morbid mood by listing dozens of past wrongs. All you need is one or two to begin this discipline. Try to ignore the wrongs done by others and stick with your own. Avoid thinking, "Well, they were wrong in that situation too." Worry more about the beam in your own eye than the speck in another's.

Gain Forgiveness First

This chapter is not directly about forgiveness and reconciliation but penance. However, if you need forgiveness, get that first before doing penance. There are excellent books on how to go about making restitution and gaining forgiveness; consult those first. If all this is too complicated to undertake this week, select another area to work on now and put the forgiveness matter on hold.

Pick a Penance Action

What act could you do to "balance the books" between you and the person or entity you wronged? Will you do a *related* action or an *unrelated* one?

Start This Week

Take your first action of penance this week. How will you know what it is like if you don't at least try it?

Think about Group Sins

Have you been a part of an entity that sinned *as a group*? If so, begin contemplating what might be done to deal with this matter. Do not rush too quickly to action, just begin pondering this week, and perhaps chat only with one other person about it.

Now What about You?

What are your specific plans to practice penance this week?

Helps for leading your class or small group through this chapter are located at the back of this book.

Part 3

The Discipline of Response

In the discipline of response, we manage our response to the experiences life brings us, both good and bad. Much—or perhaps *most*—of our spiritual growth comes as we learn to respond in a Christlike way to both difficulties and blessings. The disciplines of action and abstinence are invaluable to our spiritual progress. But if we focus only on what we do and don't do, we will miss the most powerful discipline of all—the discipline of response to life. How we respond to our enemies, suffering, material blessings, and even to marriage or divorce can advance or erode the gains we make from other spiritual disciplines. God is always forming us—not just when we are fasting or having devotions. God uses life itself as His formative tool. Our response to a searing criticism from a fellow worker can be the basis of our spiritual formation, just as fasting or prayer can be. Of course, fasting and prayer help us know how to respond rightly, so we can't dismiss all the disciplines in this book and merely "respond." A right response to life is not automatic. If anything, our natural responses are more often the wrong ones. Thus it is a spiritual *discipline* to respond the way Christ calls us to respond.

Chapter 14

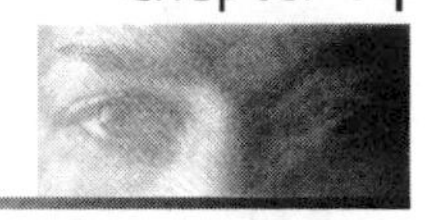

Response

4-20-08
at Lipsey's - B.S.

Consider it pure joy, my brothers, whenever you face trials of many kinds, because you know that the testing of your faith develops perseverance. Perseverance must finish its work so that you may be mature and complete, not lacking anything.

James 1:2–4

The spiritual discipline of response is managing our reactions to what life brings us—both good and bad. This concept is a novel one for a book on the spiritual disciplines, yet the discipline of response is vital. It is the third leg of the stool that supports our spiritual formation. Our character is formed by the many tiny reactions we have to bad things like opposition, suffering, pain, temptation, divorce, enemies, defeat, persecution, the death of a loved one, and even our own impending death. Similarly, we are changed by how we respond to good things such as wealth, power, promotion, favor, opportunity, or success. We do not respond to these things in a single moment. Over time we make hundreds of little responses, and they come to form us spiritually. Practicing the disciplines of action and abstinence helps us develop Christian responses, yet responding is a discipline in itself. It is more natural to respond to success by attributing it to our own cleverness than to give others the glory—thus it is a *discipline*. The response may be in what we say, how we act, or in the attitudes we develop in our thoughts—but we are responding a thousand times every day. Each of our responses becomes a thread that weaves together the rope of our character. Our character is the sum and total of our choices. In the spiritual discipline of response, we braid into that rope Christlike responses to life's situations.

Bad Things and Good People

Practicing the discipline of response develops the habit of using life experiences as a curriculum for spiritual growth. We learn to see both blessings and difficulties as the course outline for our spiritual development. Christians who take this approach are just as likely to be shocked at being diagnosed with cancer as anyone else. But Christians practicing this discipline soon begin to wonder how cancer can make them better people and even how it might help them to serve others. They will fight the cancer and pray for healing, but simultaneously they will seek to respond to it in a Christlike manner. This is a hard assignment. It can't be done in a single response but must be accomplished on hundreds occasions as new oncology reports come in and new procedures are tried. This is why it is a *discipline*—responding to life's experiences is repetitive and must become habitual in order to form us. Followers of God are not exempt from tragedy. We are, however, able to face

In this you greatly rejoice, though now for a little while you may have had to suffer grief in all kinds of trials. These have come so that your faith—of greater worth than gold, which perishes even though refined by fire—may be proved genuine and may result in praise, glory and honor when Jesus Christ is revealed.

—1 Peter 1:6–7

difficult things differently. God does not reward His people for their obedience by doling out pleasant circumstances. Christians do not automatically get to skip the difficulties of life. Being a Christian is not about getting an exemption from evil—it is about having the resources to deal with evil when it comes our way.

God Using Evil

We must be careful that we don't think God inflicts these evils upon us. It is a narrow ledge to walk: seeing evil as being *used* by God yet avoiding seeing evil as being *caused* by Him. God does not send cancer to us so we'll become better people. Cancer results from the fallen condition of our world, and God is at work on earth reversing the effects of the Fall, including cancer. Eventually He will triumph. For now, however, there is evil in the world, and God allows it. Because God could prevent evil from befalling us yet chooses not to, we know that evil is allowed to exist for some purpose. God did not prompt Joseph's brothers to sell him into slavery—Satan did. Yet while the brothers meant it for evil, God was able to use Joseph's situation for good. God can use evil circumstances to produce a good result. This is why it is so important to have the right response when bad things happen to us. When we experience evil, we ought to ask, "How can God use this?" but never say, "God did this to me." So what are some of the bad things that happen to people? What are some of the bad things that have happened

> Three times I pleaded with the LORD to take it away from me. But he said to me, "My grace is sufficient for you, for my power is made perfect in weakness." Therefore I will boast all the more gladly about my weaknesses, so that Christ's power may rest on me. That is why, for Christ's sake, I delight in weaknesses, in insults, in hardships, in persecutions, in difficulties. For when I am weak, then I am strong.
>
> —2 Corinthians 12:8–10

to you? Can you see how God used those evils to accomplish something good in your life?

Temptation

Are you facing temptation? What sort of temptation? Is the devil hounding you so that you can find no relief? At every corner do you face a new onslaught so powerful you can hardly resist? How will you respond? You can either surrender to the tempter, weakening your will, or you can resist temptation and strengthen your will for future battles. Martin Luther once remarked that the best preparation for a minister-in-training is summarized in one word: temptation. God uses temptation to strengthen your will. Every time you resist, you show your fidelity to God and make resistance in the future easier. Each successful resistance builds the muscle of your will and strengthens your resolve to obey. It is up to you. Temptation brings the opportunity to either weaken or strengthen your will. The Christian response to temptation is resistance.

Opposition

Are you doing what you know to be the right thing but find someone opposing you? Have you been doing your best yet been told it isn't good enough? Perhaps there is a whole group of people opposed to you. They turn your success into failure, your words into jokes, and dismiss you as a "featherweight mind." Perhaps no matter what you attempt, your opponents turn your accomplishments into dust. How will you respond? You can respond by simply giving up, or you can let God use this opposition to develop perseverance in you. Without opposition, how can you develop determination? It is up to you. Opposition brings the opportunity to either develop perseverance or give up. The Christian response is to persevere.

Enemies

An enemy is not just someone who opposes you but someone who is truly out to destroy you. Do you have an enemy? If so, how will you respond? You can respond by fighting back and getting even or by letting God use your enemy to develop love in you. Without an enemy, how will you ever develop the kind of selfless love that Jesus had? Even the non-Christians love their friends. Christians love their enemies—and even pray for them. Christians forgive their enemies—before they've been asked to. It is up to you. An enemy brings the opportunity to either fight back or love. The Christian response is to love.

Rejection

Did your father reject you? Or your mother? Did a friend or spouse walk away from you, discarding you like a candy wrapper? Did a group of people reject you so that you still feel the sting? How will you respond? You can respond with anger, resentment, and self-deprecation, or you can let God use your rejection to develop a sweet spirit in you. How is it that the sweetest people often have experienced the most crushing blows? The crushing lets the sweet scent of Christ escape. Without rejection you are unlikely to develop this sweet spirit. It is up to you. Rejection brings the opportunity to express either sourness or sweetness. The Christian response to rejection is to identify with Christ's own rejection, allowing His character to be displayed.

> Difficult times have helped me to understand better than before how infinitely rich and beautiful life is in every way, and that so many things that one goes worrying about are of no importance whatsoever.
>
> —Isak Dinesen

Division

Are you a part of a family or fellowship that seems hopelessly divided? Are your associates at the office or workplace at odds and alienated from each other? How will you respond? You can respond by taking sides in the dispute, or God can use that division to help you learn to be a peacemaker. Without conflict we are unlikely to ever develop peacemaking skills. It is up to you. Division and strife bring the opportunity either to join in the fray or to learn to be a peacemaker. Which will you choose? The Christian response is neither to join the battle nor to stand aloof, but to bring the sides together for reconciliation.

Injustice

Are you a victim of injustice? Are you an injured party? How will you respond? You can respond by nursing that injury until it grows into a full-blown grudge and turns you into a bitter person, or you can let God use that injustice to develop a forgiving spirit in your heart. Without experiencing injustice, we are unlikely to learn forgiveness. It is up to you. Your injury presents a fork in the road: one leading down the blind alley of bitterness, the other leading into the garden of grace and forgiveness. The Christian response is to forgive and let God collect on the debt of injustice.

Suffering

Are you facing suffering? Is your mind constantly preoccupied with your pain? Do you wonder why others seem to have no pain and face no misery like yours? How will you respond? You can respond by doubting God's goodness and mercy, or you can develop a deeper faith in God and a greater willingness to trust Him. Without suffering we will undoubtedly develop only a moderate trust in God. It is easier to believe God is good when life is good. However, a Christian proclaims God's goodness when life is bad. It is up to you. Suffering brings the opportunity for either doubt or faith, either suspicion or trust. The Christian response to suffering is to develop increased faith in God and trust in His goodness.

Failure

Have you failed miserably? Did you take a risk but it didn't pan out? Have you failed in business? Marriage? Life? Have you failed God? How will you respond? You can respond to failure by giving up and running away or by letting God use your failure to develop greater reliance on Him. Without failure we are unlikely to develop full reliance on God—we will rely on ourselves. The Christian response to failure is greater trust in the Lord.

Death

Are you facing death? Do you know that your exit from this life is looming? How will you respond? You can respond by surrendering to doubt and despair, or you can make your final days become your ultimate statement of faith. You can be either an example of doubt at death's door or an example of faith. Without facing death, we never know for certain the surety of our faith. It is up to you. Facing death is the final exam of faith. The Christian response to death is to recognize that it has no permanent sting—for we have eternal life.

> Character is a victory, not a gift.
>
> —Anonymous

Tragedy

Have you lost a parent or spouse in a tragic accident? A son or daughter? Was it some tragedy you can't understand? Has life been unfair? Do you start each day mourning your loss? Is this tragedy your last thought at night as you drift off to sleep? Has your loss

> Talent develops in tranquility, character in the full current of human life.
>
> —Goethe

come to define who you are? How will you respond? You can respond with doubt and misgivings about God that may lead you eventually to reject Him, or you can allow God to sooth the agony of tragedy in your life, extracting from you a tenderness toward others who are in pain. We develop tenderness for others as we process our own pain. It is up to you. Personal tragedy presents a choice either to head down the road of despair or to let God develop tenderness within us. The Christian response is to let God create a tender spirit within us.

Good Things and Good People

We tend to think of bad experiences as being more powerful in shaping us than good ones. At least we hear more testimonies about that sort of shaping. Yet our blessings offer an equal opportunity to respond in a way that forms us spiritually. In fact, without experiencing some blessings we will never develop some Christlike qualities.

Power

Do you have power over others? Are you in leadership? Do you teach and have the power of awarding grades in your hand? Are you a parent? If you have power, how will you respond to it? You can exercise your power like a despot, or you can temper your power with mercy. Unless we have power, we may never learn true meekness or exercise true mercy. It takes power to be meek or merciful. The Christian response to power is to learn mercy and meekness.

Success

Do others consider you successful? Do you think so too? Do you "have it made"? How will you respond? Will you take credit for your success and assume that less successful people are simply lazy, stupid, or unmotivated? Or will you use success as an opportunity to learn humility and gratefulness? The blessing of success can teach you how to be humble, giving others credit for their part in your victory. Success also presents an opportunity to become prideful, taking all credit for yourself. It is your choice. Success can make you an arrogant, self-reliant person who judges everyone else as deficient. Or it can make you a more humble and grateful person. Without success we Christians may not fully learn to be humble, grateful, and compassionate.

Supernatural Touch

Have you had a miraculous spiritual experience from God? Has He healed you, given you impressive spiritual gifts, or delivered you from some bondage? How will you respond? You could respond with spiritual pride and condemnation toward those who are so spiritually "deficient" that they have not reached the level of spirituality that you have. Or you can respond the Christian way—by giving credit to God alone for your spiritual condition and humbly treating others with dignity and respect. The choice is yours.

> There's no disaster that can't become a blessing, and no blessing that can't become a disaster.
>
> —Richard Bach

Wealth

Are you rich? Certainly there are others who are richer than you, but how many people are poorer? Does your annual income place you in the top 20 percent of the world's people? If so, you have a choice. You can respond to this blessing by hoarding your treasure, constantly investing it to build "bigger barns" for yourself, or you can open your hand and let your blessing of wealth serve others. The choice is yours.

Health

Sickness and suffering can be a means of growth if we respond to them properly, but so can health. Are you healthy? Will you learn to express daily gratitude to God for your life's vigor, or will you forget this discipline and never value your health until you lose it? The choice is yours—every day.

The All-Day Discipline

Many of the disciplines of action and abstinence can be practiced at a set time. We can schedule our devotions for 6:00 a.m. or plan a day of fasting and solitude this Saturday. The discipline of response, however, must be practiced all day long. Wrong or right attitudes are not developed in an instant—they are the products of our consistent thought patterns repeated over days, weeks, and even years. Preventing wrong attitudes from developing takes a repeated discipline of laying down tracks for right thought patterns. The discipline of response requires constant effort, daily effort, even moment-by-moment effort. By learning to discipline our response to what life brings us—both good and bad—we are trained to react as Christ would and are formed into His image.

> You don't develop courage by being happy in your relationships everyday. You develop it by surviving difficult times and challenging adversity.
>
> —Barbara De Angelis

How to Begin Practicing Response

Define Your Bad Experiences

What bad situation do you now face? Identify it, even if it only seems like a little thing compared to the issues above. Ask, "If God uses bad things in my life to make me better—what are those bad things?" Most Christians can think of at least one item in their lives that is painful, difficult, or at least irritating.

Define Your Blessings

What blessings and opportunities have you received? What are the good things in your life that also require a right response if you are to become more Christlike? Both these lists make ideal subjects to be recorded in your journal.

Describe the Choice

When encountering any difficulty or blessing, we face a choice. Describe this choice, this fork in the road—the two possible responses, one leading away from Christ, the other toward Him.

Determine to Choose Right

Decide that you *will* make the right choice in the many individual responses to your difficulties and blessings. All these little decisions make you who you are—but the big, initial decision gets you started on the path to using life's good and bad things to make you better.

Get Accountability

The discipline of response is not a one-time event. It is an ongoing discipline. Find someone to check up on you frequently and monitor your success in learning to see both blessings and difficulty as a means of grace.

Now What about You?

What are your specific plans to practice the discipline of response this week?

Helps for leading your class or small group through this chapter are located at the back of this book.

The Problem with This Book

If you skipped ahead to read this conclusion as a shortcut, that could be a sign of your own lack of discipline and need for the book you just skipped. However, if you have read the book (or at least most of it) this chapter will be helpful by raising some cautions about the spiritual disciplines. There are limitations and dangers in practicing personal spiritual disciplines. While the disciplines discussed in this book are a powerful means of grace that God uses to change us, any blessing can become a curse if treated wrongly. If you have been delighted at your progress in the spiritual disciplines and feel you've gotten a grip on these secrets of holy living, this chapter is written for you. It outlines the dangers you'll soon face.

A Caution on Self-Centeredness

Preoccupation with the personal disciplines can lead to a preoccupation with self. Certainly God wants us to draw closer to Him and to take advantage of the disciplines that put us into the channels of His grace, but it is possible to love the disciplines more than we love others and the church. It is even possible to love the disciplines more than we love Christ. The spiritual disciplines, if loved too much, can become the end and not the means of grace. God calls us to be close to Him, but He also calls us to participate in the church and to do His work in the world. People who become enamored with slipping away from others to be with the Lord might just love being with themselves more than being with God. The personal spiritual disciplines do help us get closer to God. But we have all of eternity to draw closer to God yet only one short life to do His work on earth. We must avoid the error of some monks—becoming so absorbed with the first Great Commandment that we forget the second.

Spiritual Self-Sufficiency

Once we develop a disciplined life, we might assume that we have mastered the means of grace and know the secret recipe for holiness. We may begin to think we can become holy merely by having devotions, scheduling fasts, practicing simplicity, and keeping our journals up to date. While the spiritual disciplines are indeed channels of God's grace, they do not dispense grace themselves. There is no spiritual power in fasting. There is no changing power in prayer, confession, or even the Bible. If we believe the disciplines themselves make us holy, we have made an idol of them. The disciplines are a *channel* for God's grace. The power always comes from God; it merely passes through these disciplines. A river only carries water; it does not produce it. If we love the disciplines too much, we may rely on them and not on God. Worse, when we do this, we are actually relying on *ourselves*—on *our* discipline—to become holy. Relying on self destroys us spiritually. Thus, those who practice these disciplines must never see them as anything more than a river of God's grace that we may enter into and be cleaned. Loving the spiritual disciplines is good. Loving God and others is better.

Spiritual Elitism

Practicing the spiritual disciplines can make us feel spiritually superior to others. One of the reasons we like the spiritual disciplines is that they are outward signs of spirituality. They are measurable. We can count the number of days we fasted. We can see how worn and underlined our Bibles have become. We can keep a tiny card in our wallet testifying to our generosity, even if the actual giving was done in secret. We can keep track of how much time we spend in devotions each day and feel good about it. When we tally these little markers of spirituality, we impress ourselves. We are amazed at how far we've come, how much we've grown, how stable and strong we've turned out to be. We wish others could discover the power in this sort of life. We wish the young people could at least get started on a journey like this. We thank God that He has led us to discover these practices. We thank Him that He guided us step by step as we developed the disciplined life. We give Him all the credit for our progress, thanking Him that we are not like others—those still living undisciplined and immature spiritual lives. We praise God because we've escaped that shallow and unreliable life and are no longer guided by our emotions. We begin praying for revival: "O Lord, please raise up a generation of Christians who are willing to pay the price to become like me." And we pray ourselves right into *spiritual pride*! We must remember that the most spiritually disciplined people of Jesus' day were not His disciples but the Pharisees. They practiced these disciplines well. Pride of any kind is repugnant to God, but spiritual pride is the worst variety. The devil is always prepared to tempt us and will use whatever is at hand—even our close relationship to God. Remember, Satan fell from a place near the very throne of God. Yes, we ought to practice the spiritual disciplines. But they ought to make us more humble. They ought to teach us to think of others as better than ourselves—even spiritually. If practicing the disciplines has inflated our opinion of ourselves, we have missed their point. It is our opinion of God that needs to be inflated.

Individualism

Perhaps the greatest danger of all in practicing the spiritual disciplines is that we might come to believe that the Christian life is solitary—just between God and me. This false notion is already too popular in the Western world. Individualism was alien to the New Testament church and to the religion of the Old Testament as well. We moderns believe in personal fulfillment, personal conversion, personal devotions, a personal relationship with Jesus Christ, and the personal spiritual disciplines covered in this book. These are all good, but they are only half of the picture. The other half is *others*. Others includes the church, which is the body of Christ, and the world for whom Christ died. Our individualistic bias is so strong that it affects even how we read the Bible. For instance, when we see the word *you*, we immediately assume the *you* means *me*—me personally, the individual me. Yet most of the *you's* in the Bible that we take individually are actually plural—addressed to a group of people, not to each of us personally. We forget that the Bible was addressed to real groups of people. There really were Corinthians, Colossians, and Ephesians, just as there are now New Yorkers, Canadians, and Australians. And most of the Bible was written to various groups of people.

The early Christians did not have personal copies of these books to read or study in their homes. They *heard* these books read aloud when they gathered for worship. They heard the Bible collectively rather than reading it individually. So the *you's* in Paul's epistles, for example, were heard as instructions to the entire church—a plural use of the word *you*. Our modern, individualized minds have little room for this sort of thinking. We see the church as a locker room where individuals prepare for what is really important—living our personal life from Monday through Saturday. That is both bad theology and a bad understanding of Scripture. And it was alien to the church when it first read the Bible. Thus, when we read the Apostle Paul's most famous verse on spiritual formation, "My dear children, for whom I am again in the pains of childbirth until Christ is formed in you" (Gal. 4:19), we apply it individually—as if spiritual formation is a solitary matter that is "all about me." However, the *you* is plural. The verse was written to "you all"—a group of churches in Asia Minor. Paul was writing about the church—all of the people in it—becoming the body of Christ. It was about the spiritual formation of a group, not a person. Personal spiritual formation is indeed important, and this whole book has been about that subject. But personal formation is only half the story. The rest of the story is the corporate spiritual formation of the church. Spiritual formation is about making a holy people, not just holy persons. If we become fixated on personal spiritual disciplines, we are likely to miss the collective nature of spiritual formation. God wants more than to make a few people here and there into saints. He wants to make His church, collectively, a holy people.

Solitary Christianity

None of us can be Christ's body alone. If the church is to be a witness to the world, it will be as the "parts" gather and form the body of Christ. The gathered believers are the body of Christ. Scattered, we are, at best, disconnected body parts. None of us will ever have all of the qualities or the total perfection of Jesus Christ. Yet as we gather, we find one person who illustrates Christ's mercy almost perfectly and another who comes close to Christ's compassion. Still another seems to illustrate Christ's sense of justice. Only when we are gathered, experiencing life together, do we display the fullness of Christ's character. Too much emphasis on the personal spiritual disciplines can lead us to think we don't need the church—that the Christian life is a solitary one. The truth is that we cannot be fully Christian apart from the body of Christ. We find His body only in the church—not in individual Christians, no matter how spiritual they may be. The church as the body of Christ is more than a theoretical construct of all individual believers that never actually gathers (the Church Invisible). The body of Christ is a visible gathering of believers. If we want to see the body of Christ today, our search will always lead us to a physical gathering of believers that we call a church. So rather than making us spiritually independent, the right use of the spiritual disciplines should make us increasingly dependent on the other parts of Christ's body. As we draw closer to Christ through the disciplines, we will be drawn closer to His body. If not, our spiritual disciplines are being used by Satan and not God. While the disciplines might lead us away from others for a time, they always lead us back to the visible body of Christ that exists on earth today—the church of Jesus Christ.

Bridal Mysticism

Just as we cannot be the body of Christ alone, we cannot be the bride of Christ by ourselves. The *bride of Christ* is another term for the church, one that emphasizes the purity of God's people. The bride of Christ is the church, sanctified by Christ in order to present it to himself "without spot or blemish." Practicing the spiritual disciplines can lead us wrongly on this point if we are not careful. The intimacy with God produced by these disciplines can lead to a kind of spirituality sometimes called *bridal mysticism*. In this form of spirituality, individuals come to imagine that their personal relationship with Christ is like that of a bride to a groom. This sort of walk with Christ has even had erotic overtones at times throughout history. Today it might be referred to as "Jesus-is-my-boyfriend religion." It is a relationship with Jesus that borders on having an invisible perfect friend or, for some, an ideal husband. Jesus was indeed a real man, a human being who lived on this earth. But thinking of our role as the bride of

Christ as an individual rather than a corporate relationship misses the mark of New Testament teaching and can lead to psychological maladies. Jesus is the groom for the church collective, not for anyone personally. Any Christian who eliminates two thirds of the Trinity and focuses all devotional life on Jesus alone is in danger of such error. God is the Father, Son, and Holy Spirit. Making Jesus-the-man into an invisible, ideal boyfriend is not spiritual intimacy but spiritual sacrilege. The bride of Christ is a group of people—the church. Any time our spiritual intimacy is invested in Jesus alone, without the Father and Spirit, we may be treading close to bridal mysticism.

As repugnant as that error is, there is one danger even greater. That is believing that our own spiritual life is the most important matter to God. What God seeks is intimacy with the church—the people of God, the bride of Christ—not just Christians as individuals. We can never satisfy God's need for a bride. Only a group can do this—His church. Thus our personal spiritual disciplines should never detract from our commitment to the *collective* spiritual disciplines of the church. If the personal spiritual disciplines make us love the church any less, they are not a means of grace but of damnation.

The Next Steps

It might be said that practicing the spiritual disciplines puts us "under the spout where the grace comes out." That is, by getting in the channel where God's grace ordinarily flows, we become changed people. Through fasting, prayer, Scripture reading, simplicity, silence, penance, confession, and the other disciplines, God will transform our thoughts, words, and deeds. As God pours His grace on us, it will cleanse us from the pollution of the world. We will gain wisdom from the Scriptures, and we'll have new insight into life. We will be able to see solutions to problems, which others miss. We will experience serenity and find purpose in life we'd never dreamed of.

So, why does God do all this in us? Is it even for *us* at all? Yes, but these benefits and insights are meant to be shared with others as well. Our serenity lets us advise the frantic. Our purpose enables us to lead the aimless. Our knowledge of the Scriptures helps us teach believers. The difficulties we have faced help us minister to those facing similar trials. Our victories enable us to warn others who are similarly blessed. Our triumphs and defeats become our curriculum for teaching others. We may have forgotten this old song, but we would do well to recapture its words—"Others, Lord, yes, others, let this our motto be." The path to true holiness may lead away from others momentarily, but it always returns to others so we can freely pass on what we have freely received.

Passing It On

So how do we pass on to others what we gain from the spiritual disciplines? We give our time. God often changes people through other people. We can be His tools to spiritually form others. So where do we start? We start with one other person, perhaps our spouse, our child, or a friend at work. We may call this *mentoring* or something else; it doesn't matter. The person might be aware of what is happening or they may not think we are doing anything more than becoming friends. Yet we become a spiritual mentor, passing on to others the benefits we have received from drawing closer to God. We give our time to them. We believe in them. We meet with them. We turn the conversation to spiritual things and learn to ask the right kind of questions. We do not try to make them become like us. We try to help them become like Christ. We invest what we gained from our solitary moments into the lives of others. Then God multiplies our investment and makes it fruitful. We see others changed. This is mentoring.

Or we might join a *small group* of four or five or ten. In this men's accountability breakfast, student Bible study, or women's prayer group, we find a place to minister to others with the wisdom we gained while alone with God. Or we might be challenged to teach a *large class* at our church, where our biblical understanding and wisdom can be passed on to others.

Whatever we do, we invest our treasure and do not bury it in the ground. We see God change lives as a result. This is what God does with His people—uses them as channels of change in the lives of others. We will be astonished at how much God uses us. People will tell us they sense God's presence in us. They will recognize God's wisdom in our words. They might think we are just smart, but we will know better. We will now that our wisdom is God. As we continually pour our time into others, we become instruments in God's hands for their spiritual formation. God molds others through us. This is what the disciplines are for—we receive from God, then give to others. In the beginning, the disciplines are channels of God grace to us, but in the end, we become a means of grace to others. What a wonderful plan! How does all this happen? It happens mostly within the body of Christ—the church. In the body of Christ, we find opportunities to be channels of God's grace to others.

Group Spiritual Formation

This book on the personal spiritual disciplines may be helpful in getting us started on the journey to deeper Christian living, but it is only a start. For the journey leads soon back into the church. We may have drawn closer to God in studying and practicing these personal spiritual disciplines, but we have ignored here the *collective* spiritual disciplines. Just as there are individual disciplines that help a person get closer to God, there are collective disciplines that help form Christ in a group—the church. What would happen if an entire church committed itself to spiritual formation *as a group*, just as individuals here and there have done with the study of this book? Have you ever tried to light one piece of charcoal? It is difficult. Even if you do get it lit, it usually goes out quickly if it stands alone. Individuals who practice the spiritual disciplines are like that single piece of charcoal. However, when a church pursues the collective spiritual disciplines, it is like lighting a heap of charcoal—the spiritual heat lasts as each coal generates fire in the others. We should never consider the personal disciplines to be the end of the road. This road always leads back into the church, where we can be spiritually formed as a group to become the visible body of Christ on earth. In this book we studied the personal spiritual disciplines. We must also think about the corporate spiritual disciplines. And these are the topics the second book in this series will address.

Helps for leading your class or small group through this chapter are located at the back of this book.

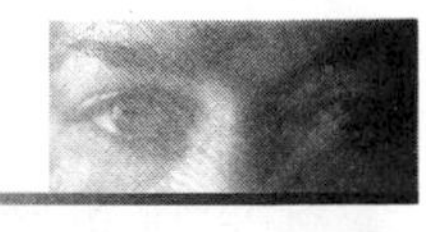

[illegible]tudy Guide

How to Le[illegible]ng from This Book

This book is [illegible] iplines, but it is best studied in comm[illegible] Sunday school class. The basic outline fo[illegible]g from this book includes these elements.

1. *Opening caring/sharing time*. Spend a few minutes catching up on one another's lives and praying together.
2. *Accountability*. Ask everyone to report on what we all did to try last week's discipline.
3. *Teacher Introduction*. Give a brief summary of summary of important points from the current week's chapter.
4. *Bible Study*. Read at least one of the scriptures mentioned in the chapter and deal with the questions in this section that relate to it.
5. *Discussion*. Select (or have group members suggest) questions from this section and discuss them with the group.
6. *Application and Reflection*. Allow silence while each person writes a response to the final question—"What are your plans for trying this discipline this week?" Don't skip this part, ever. If your group has developed a high level of trust, you might allow members to announce their goals.
7. *Prayer*. Pray together, asking God to direct your efforts and reveal himself during the next week.

It is important that you focus this book on actually trying the disciplines and not merely studying them. Make the group about *life change*, not merely about gaining knowledge. Learning more about prayer is nice, but it will be of little use unless we actually pray more. Knowing about the value of solitude is not enough—we need to spend time alone. Be at peace with the idea that students will try a new discipline each week and then move on. This study introduces us to a variety of means of grace, and we can't practice all of them all the time.

During your group's last session together, consider including a time where you consider your commitment to practicing these disciplines over the next six months. That will encourage everyone to select a few disciplines to practice on a more permanent basis.

Until then let each week be a wonderful exploratory time as you experiment with new ways of getting closer to God as individuals and then share your experience with the group.

Chapter 1: Fasting

1. Read the quote by Russel M. Nelson on page 14. When steel is tempered, the metal is heated and then cooled so that it becomes stronger than metal that has need faced the heat. How might fasting "temper" a Christian?

   Do you think there may be a connection between the sensory desires for food and other cravings? That is, how might fasting help us overcome other appetites?

2. Refer to the scripture from Matthew 4 on page 15. Would it have been wrong for Jesus to turn stone into bread? Why or why not?

   Fasting and prayer are often companions in the Bible. How would you relate Scripture and fasting?

3. Can you see any connection between doing without food as we fast and feeling grateful to God? If so, what is it?

4. Read Glen Argan's comment on page 17. Considering our culture at

large, to what other things do we have an "inordinate attachment" that might be addressed by fasting?

5. Based on Andrew Murray's observation (see page 19), to whom does fasting show the deepness of our commitment? To God? Ourselves? Why is this important?

6. Fasting is a mortal blow to the temporal, material world. Looking at the table of contents for this book, ask, "What other disciplines refocus our lives from the temporal to the spiritual?"

7. Read Isaiah 58:6–7 (page 16). While Israel was fasting, what more important duties were they overlooking? List them.

   Do you think it is OK for people to start fasting even though they may be generally uninvolved in caring for these "weightier matters"?

8. In each case below, label the kind of fast mentioned and its purpose:

   "Moses was there with the LORD forty days and forty nights without eating bread or drinking water. And he wrote on the tablets the words of the covenant—the Ten Commandments" (Exod. 34:28).

   "They mourned and wept and fasted till evening for Saul and his son Jonathan, and for the army of the LORD and the house of Israel, because they had fallen by the sword" (2 Sam. 1:12).

   "David pleaded with God for the child. He fasted and went into his house and spent the nights lying on the ground" (2 Sam. 12:16).

   "On the twenty-fourth day of the same month, the Israelites gathered together, fasting and wearing sackcloth and having dust on their heads" (Neh. 9:1).

   "[Anna] never left the temple but worshiped night and day, fasting and praying" (Luke 2:37).

   "Paul and Barnabas appointed elders for them in each church and, with prayer and fasting, committed them to the Lord, in whom they had put their trust" (Acts 14:23).

9. What will you do to begin practicing fasting this week?

Chapter 2: Silence

1. Based on Henri Nouwen's observation (see page 25), how do silence and solitude relate? Which is more dependent on the other?

2. Look in the table of contents of this book, then relate other disciplines of spiritual formation to silence. Which disciplines best form an alloy with silence? Why?

3. According to Dallas Willard (see page 24), of what does silence strip us? What are some other reasons silence might frighten us?

4. Read Henri Nouwen's comment on page 24. List some situations in which nothing may be the best thing to say.

5. What are the signals you can give to show you are actively listening—that you really care and have compassion?

6. Thomas Merton suggests that silence enables us to love others more, but not for their words (see the quote on page 27). What do people say that causes you to like them?

   How might times of silence spent alone affect our time of companionship with others?

7. Read Psalm 46:10. Why is it hard for us to be still in our world? What values resist stillness?

8. Consider the quote by Ausonius on page 26. In what ways should being silent alone change how we speak when we return to our companions?

9. The Quakers popularized the use of silence during worship to listen to God. Modern worship fills the service with words and music so that few worshipers have time for contemplation or listening for God. How could worship be changed to provide some times for listening for God's "still small voice?"

   What problems or resistance would you anticipate if your ideas were actually implemented in worship at your local church?

10. What is the danger of placing too much emphasis on listening personally to God?

11. What will you do to begin practicing silence this week?

Chapter 3: Solitude

1. Refer to the scriptures on pages 32 and 34. According to these verses, at what times did Jesus seek solitude?

   Read Luke 4:42 (page 31). Do you think Luke is suggesting that Jesus was fleeing the crowd? If so, why might he have done so? Why do we need to flee the crowd at times? What happens when we don't?

   How often do you think Jesus practiced the discipline of solitude?

2. Prayer seems often to be connected with solitude. How can being alone enhance prayer?

3. According to Paul Tillich, there is a distinct difference between loneliness and solitude (see page 32). What do you think the differences are between loneliness and being alone?

   In what way can solitude actually help banish one's loneliness?

4. Based on the observation by Thomas à Kempis on page 34, how is peace related to solitude?

   The hermits and monks had "cells" where they found solitude. What might be a modern equivalent to the monk's cell?

5. Read the quote by Thomas Merton on page 33. What are today's chief diversions that tend to draw us away from time with God?

   What are the dangers of collectivity as opposed to the solitary life? What could be the dangers of a solitary life?

6. For a modern person, how much time should be spent alone with God in order to create balance?

7. Are some people called to a solitary life of prayer and study while others have minimal obligation to solitude?

8. What will you do to begin practicing solitude this week?

Chapter 4: Simplicity

1. Read the quote by Edwin Way Teale on page 39. List some examples of situations when "eliminating needless wants" could reduce work or worry? Have new possessions ever increased your work or worry?

2. Reflect on the quote by John Burroughs on page 38. Describe some simple things that bring you joy?

3. Read Hans Hofmann's comment on page 45. What are the necessary things that we should be tuned in to that we miss when drowning in a materialistic life?

   In what ways does the clutter of possessions block you from tuning in to important things?

4. Richard Foster states that we should impress people with our lives and not with our clothes (see the quote on page 39). Could there be an inverse relationship between the two ways we impress people—that is, the more we impress them by how we dress or what we have, the less they see who we really are? Can you think of a story that illustrates this idea?

   What are the best possible impressions a person can get from your clothes? From your life? Make two lists and compare them.

5. Read the quote by Charles Dudley Warner on page 40. Make a list of the possessions you would have if you lived your life with "just baggage enough."

6. Why do humans collect possessions? How do you explain this universal tendency?

7. Refer to the scripture from Matthew 6 on page 43. Is this an absolute command like "Do not steal," or is it more relative? That is, would it be accurate to interpret the command this way: "As you store up treasure on earth, make sure you're also storing up treasure in heaven"? If you think it is, then do you also think we should interpret Jesus' other "do not" statements in a similar way? If you think this is an absolute command, then how do you think it should be applied to our lives today?

Do our hearts follow our treasure, or does our treasure follow our hearts? If you have your heart set on your possessions, how do you go about changing it? Should you change your heart first (and count on your treasure following your heart), or should you start putting your treasure in heaven (and count on your heart to follow it)? Try to avoid the easy answer, "It's both," when answering these questions.

8. Read Matthew 6:24 (page 44). Is Jesus saying that we shouldn't care about money at all, or is He saying that we should devote 51 percent or more of our services to God and not to our money? What percentage meets this command of Christ in your mind? What would constitute disobedience of this teaching?

9. Few can take up the ascetic life, as John the Baptist did (read Matthew 3:4 on page 45). However, there are some people today who live a life of radical simplicity. Can you think of anyone like this?

   Could you live a life of radical simplicity for even one week, or maybe for one month? How would you go about it?

10. What will you do to begin practicing simplicity this week?

Chapter 5: Rest

1. Reflect on Etty Hilsum's comment on rest (see page 51). What are some practices that give you momentary rest in the midst of a hectic day? List them.

2. Read Psalm 23:1–3 (page 52). When have you experienced rest in "green pastures"? Has God ever made you lie down, or forced you to rest?

3. According to John Steinbeck, a problem can often be solved by "sleeping on it" (read the quote on page 51). Give an example of a time when you awoke to find a problem resolved.

   What role might the Holy Spirit play in working with our unconscious minds while we sleep?

   What healthy role can dreaming accomplish?

4. Read Matthew 11:28–29 on page 53. When we go to Christ for rest, what kind of rest will He supply? How?

   Jesus says He is "gentle and humble in heart." Can you see any possible connection with these qualities and rest?

5. Read Thomas Dekker's comment on page 53. There is ample evidence of physical maladies being brought on or worsened by going without sleep. How might a Christian treat rest as a stewardship issue?

6. Refer to the scripture from Genesis 2 on page 50. Discuss how Sunday was treated in your home when you were growing up.

   Can we have a Sabbath that is not held on the original day (Saturday) or even Sunday?

   What do you do to set aside one day of your week as a day of rest?

7. Jesus once slept through a violent storm, while he was on a boat (see Matt. 8:24 on page 52). What sorts of things cause you to be as exhausted as Jesus apparently was in this story?

   Tell about a time when you fell asleep when others were wide awake.

   Make a list of all the clever places and times you can think of to take a nap in the midst of a busy day.

8. What makes it so hard to rest? What are the arguments we make against sleeping and resting?

9. Read Benjamin Franklin's comment on page 51. Do you think there is an inverse relationship between greatness and rest—meaning that the greater we suppose we are, the harder it is to rest and that the lower our self-esteem, the more we feel obligated to "stay up and catch up"?

10. Read Psalm 91:1 on page 55. How can we "hide" in God's shadow?

11. Review the Christian disciplines listed in the table of contents of this book. Can you connect rest with any of the other disciplines? Which are the most compatible with rest? Which may actually detract from rest?

12. What will you do to begin practicing rest this week?

Chapter 6: Secrecy

1. Read Matthew 6:4, 6, and 18 (page 60). Do these verses mean that we don't have to wait until we get to heaven to get credit—that we will be rewarded here and now?

   Some people have used these verses to support their idea of not advertising their church, instead letting God draw the people He has selected to them. What do you think of this idea?

   How might God bring an open reward for a secret service? Give some examples of how this might work.

2. Read the quote by Dallas Willard on page 60. How far should people go to obscure their piety?

3. Refer to the scripture from Matthew 5 on page 61. This verse, in which Jesus teaches his disciples to let their good deeds be seen by others so they will bring glory to the Father, is located just one chapter before Jesus' warning to avoid doing good deeds in order to be seen by others. How can we bring these two seemingly contradictory teachings together?

   How can we make sure we give glory to God and not to ourselves when others see our good deeds or gifts?

   If someone asked you for tips on how to follow this teaching, what would you say?

4. Reflect on the comments by Thomas à Kempis (page 62) and the unnamed Desert Father (page 64). What reasonable actions could you take to prevent others from praising your practice of spiritual disciplines or your good deeds?

   What effect does praise have on people?

   How might praise be both beneficial and harmful?

5. Read Matthew 6:3–4 (page 63). Our giving cannot always be kept a secret, yet what are some things a church might do to avoid catering to a person's desire for praise for giving and serving?

   Do you think these verses mean that we should refrain from thanking others for their generosity or acts of service?

6. Refer to the scripture from John 7 on page 59. In what way were the brothers of Jesus acting as His public relations agent?

   Do you think their advice makes sense?

   How did the brothers misunderstand Christ's mission?

   How do their assumptions figure in our own hopes for success and recognition?

7. Read Philippians 2:3–4 (page 65). Describe a good act that could be done out of selfish ambition.

   What is vain conceit? How does it figure into the notion of letting good deeds be seen by others?

8. What will you do to begin practicing secrecy this week?

Chapter 7: Journaling

1. Read the quotes by Isabel Allende and Virginia Woolf on page 70. Write down some of the good things God has done for you in the last year.

2. Refer to the scripture from Deuteronomy 27 on page 70. The stones set up by the Israelites upon crossing the Jordan were meant to remind them of their deliverance and to be a testimony to their children of God's faithfulness. In the same way, your journal will preserve a record of God's faithfulness for your children and grandchildren. But how might you protect them from the private thoughts you share only with God?

3. What wisdom do the quotes by Peter De Vries and Erasmus (see pages 72) offer on the discipline of journaling?

4. Read Deuteronomy 10:2 (page 74). Imagine what might have happened if the Ten Commandments had not been written down and kept.

   What do you think Christianity would be like if we did not have the Bible?

5. What do you wish you knew about the spiritual lives of your grandparents or great grandparents?

6. Read Revelation 1:19 (page 75)
7. Do you think John fully understood the meaning of the vision he recorded in Revelation?

   Does God still give people premonitions or prophecies concerning the future? What might be some advantages or disadvantages of writing them down?
8. What will you do to begin practicing journaling this week?

Chapter 8: Hospitality

1. Reflect on the quote by Christine Pohl on page 82. Describe how we might entertain people at our home yet never share our lives and ourselves.
2. Read the quote by Max Beerbohm on page 83. What does it mean to turn hospitality into an "art"?

   Most classic writers on hospitality disparage fancy busyness that is designed to impress guests, but what would you say to someone who loves "making a fuss" when entertaining others?
3. The quote by O. Henry on page 85 accurately represents the value of hospitality to those in the ancient world, who actually did entertain their enemies. Hospitality was so rooted in the culture that it trumped killing an enemy—or at least preceded it. And Jesus taught us to do good to our enemies. Do you have enemies? How might you be hospitable to them?

   If your church were to invite a group of people who were like "enemies" to a dinner, who would that group be?
4. Based on the poem by Thomas Bailey Aldrich on page 81, how can you know that a guest feels comfortable in your home?

   What are some ways to make guests feel they are at home and no longer guests in your home?
5. Refer to the scripture from Luke 10 on page 84. Are you more inclined to act like Mary or Martha?

What are the strengths and weaknesses of each style?

From Jesus' point of view, what was wrong with Martha's approach to hosting?

6. For each of the following scriptural references to hospitality, answer the two following questions: What words are used to recommend hospitality? To what kind of person, word, or concept is hospitality related in this verse?

   "Share with God's people who are in need. Practice hospitality" (Rom. 12:13).

   "Now the overseer must be above reproach, the husband of but one wife, temperate, self-controlled, respectable, hospitable, able to teach, not given to drunkenness, not violent but gentle, not quarrelsome, not a lover of money" (1 Tim. 3:2).

   "No widow may be put on the list of widows unless she is over sixty, has been faithful to her husband, and is well known for her good deeds, such as bringing up children, showing hospitality, washing the feet of the saints, helping those in trouble and devoting herself to all kinds of good deed" (1 Tim. 5:9–10).

   "Since an overseer is entrusted with God's work, he must be blameless—not overbearing, not quick-tempered, not given to drunkenness, not violent, not pursuing dishonest gain. Rather he must be hospitable, one who loves what is good, who is self-controlled, upright, holy and disciplined" (Titus 1:7–8).

   "Do not forget to entertain strangers, for by so doing some people have entertained angels without knowing it" (Heb. 13:2).

   "Above all, love each other deeply, because love covers over a multitude of sins. Offer hospitality to one another without grumbling. Each one should use whatever gift he has received to serve others, faithfully administering God's grace in its various forms" (1 Pet. 4:8–10).

   "It was for the sake of the Name that they went out, receiving no help from the pagans. We ought therefore to show hospitality to such men so that we may work together for the truth" (3 John 7–8).

7. What will you do to begin practicing hospitality this week?

Chapter 9: Confession

1. How are confession, healing, and prayer connected in James 5:16 (see page 91)?

2. Read Nehemiah 9:3 (page 92). In what ways might collective confession relate to individual confession? Have you ever witnessed collective confession? Describe it.

   What are the advantages and disadvantages of collective confession in church?

3. Refer to the scripture from Acts 19 on page 93. Have you ever seen a public service of confession like that? Describe it.

   What cautions would you offer about such public confessions?

4. Read Leviticus 26:40–42 (page 96). Why would God ask people to confess the "sins of their fathers"?

   How might the practice of confessing for others apply to us?

5. Read the quote by Fulton J. Sheen on page 97. What can "good" people confess? Do you think it's possible that some people truly have nothing to confess?

6. What will you do to begin practicing confession this week?

Chapter 10: Scripture

1. God sanctifies us as He transforms us from who we were into the image of His son; He spiritually forms us. In John 17:17 (see page 103), Jesus prays for God to sanctify His followers through His Word, which is truth. In your own words, describe how the Word sanctifies us.

2. Refer to the passage from 2 Timothy 3 on page 105. For each of the four uses of scripture cited in these verses, describe how it relates to personal devotions. Give an example of how the Bible teaches, rebukes, corrects, and trains us in righteousness.

3. Read Psalm 119:15–16 (page 108). Differentiate between the terms *meditate*, *consider*, and *delight* as they relate to using the Bible.

   List some reasons why we so easily neglect the word of God.

4. In each case below, explain the value of Scripture pointed out by that specific verse:

   "Your word is a lamp to my feet and a light for my path" (Ps. 119:105).

   "I have hidden your word in my heart that I might not sin against you" (Ps. 119:11).

   "Jesus replied, 'You are in error because you do not know the Scriptures or the power of God'" (Matt. 22:29).

   "For everything that was written in the past was written to teach us, so that through endurance and the encouragement of the Scriptures we might have hope" (Rom. 15:4).

   "For the word of God is living and active. Sharper than any double-edged sword, it penetrates even to dividing soul and spirit, joints and marrow; it judges the thoughts and attitudes of the heart" (Heb. 4:12).

   What other value of Scripture would you add to this list?

5. Refer to the scripture from James 1 on page 107. James, the brother of Jesus insists that input without output is useless. Think about and then discuss the following quote by someone who disagrees with this chapter's point of view: "We have a church full of people who *know* far more than they *do*. Our problem is not that we do not know what to do—it is that we do not do what we know. We don't need more Bible study; we need more Bible action."

   What is the ideal balance between knowing and doing? Explain your answer.

   Tell about a time when your doing came after your knowing. Tell the story for others so they can borrow wisdom from your experience.

6. What will you do to begin practicing Scripture this week?

Chapter 11: Charity

1. Read Deuteronomy 15:4 and John 12:8 (see pages 114 and 119). How do these two verses relate to each other?

   According to Deuteronomy 15:4, God prefers that there be no poor among us. How do you think God plans to banish poverty?

2. Evangelicals almost always put faith before charity; however, Paul places charity as greater than faith (refer to the scripture from 1 Corinthians 13 on page 115). What will this mean to us if we take it seriously?

3. Read James 2:14–16 (page 116). How does James see faith and charity interacting?

4. Based on 1 John 3:17–18 (see page 117), draw a diagram that shows the relationship between God's love for me, my love for God and my charity to others.

5. Read James 1:27 (page 118). Who would James say that we should look after today?

6. Refer to the scripture from Matthew 25 on page 113. If you were to take this parable literally—to see giving to the poor as giving to Jesus—how might that change the way in which you practice the discipline of charity?

7. Read Acts 10:5 (see page 117). Imagine in what way Cornelius's almsgiving came up in heaven. Is this a picture of what really happens in heaven when we give to the poor?

8. Refer to the scripture from Ezekiel 16:49 on page 120. The sexual sins of Sodom are well known; however, Ezekiel highlights three other sins in this verse. List them and describe what they might look like today.

9. Read the German proverb on page 118. What are some causes of poverty? How should Christians address these causes?

   Charity gives itself rich; covetousness hoards itself poor.To what extent does "deserving" rightfully figure into our charity?

10. Discuss the meaning of the quote by Jack London on page 119.

11. Read the quote by Mother Teresa on page 120. Mother Teresa's focus was not on how many she served but on how many she missed. Imagine this approach applied to other efforts by the church such as evangelism or counting attendance. Do you think this approach is too negative?

12. Consider Dan Bennett's comment on "real charity" on page 114. If the income tax deductions for charitable giving were eliminated, do you think some people would cease to give? How would it affect your personal giving if charitable contributions were not tax deductible?

13. What will you do to begin practicing charity this week?

Chapter 12: Prayer

1. Read the quotes by R. A. Torrey and Elisabeth Elliott (pages 126 and 128) as well as Romans 8:26 (page 125). If the Holy Spirit can pray "through us," how can we open ourselves up to be channels for this kind of prayer?

   How do we know that prayer is not just talking to ourselves?
   What makes a thought a prayer?

2. Read Mark 11:25 (page 133). Diagram the relationship between forgiveness from God, another person, and yourself?

3. Luke 6:28 says that we should pray for those who mistreat us (see page 126). Who are your enemies? How, exactly, might we pray for them? Give an example of a prayer you could pray for them?

4. Refer to the scripture from Luke 5 and 6 on pages 129 and 126. How important is location to prayer? What are your criteria for finding a place of prayer?

   Does more time spent in prayer make prayer more effective? Which is more important, the frequency of prayer or its duration?

5. Some people believe prayer chains are a pagan manifestation of prayer as magic, while many others believe they are useful and powerful. What do you think would turn authentic prayer into a pagan practice?

6. Read Philippians 4:6 and the comment by Corrie Ten Boom (see pages 128 and 129). Are some things "too little" to bother God about? If so, what are they? If not, then what are the dangers of praying about "little things"?

   How do prayer and worry relate?

7. Refer to the scripture from Luke 11 on page 130. How important is persistence in prayer? When does persistence become presumption?

   Can we talk God into doing something that is bad for us?

8. After reading Matthew 21:22 (page 131), explain how you interpret this verse. How does your style of interpreting this passage apply to other verses of Scripture? What are the advantages and disadvantages of your style of interpretation?

9. Using the verses from Luke 11 on page 134, draw out principles of answered prayer.

10. What will you do to begin practicing prayer this week?

Chapter 13: Penance

1. Refer to the scripture from Hebrews 12 on page 139. How would you relate self-imposed penance and God-imposed chastening? How are they alike? How are they different?

   What self-imposed rules have you already established to discipline yourself, break bad habits, or make new habits?

2. Reflect on the quote by Beau Hummel on page 140. Since Jesus "paid it all" for us on the cross, what serious doctrinal crime do we commit if we imagine our penance somehow balances out our sins?

   Can you think of any person who might be forgiven by God but not by other people?

3. Using the story of Adam and Eve, describe the difference between forgiveness and earthly punishment.

4. Read the quote by Garnet May Anderson on page 145. How often should we remind ourselves of our sins? Can we be reminded too often?

5. Read John Leonard's comment on page 143. Make up a realistic situation in which a sin might first seem rather small but is actually quite serious.

6. Refer to the scripture from 2 Samuel 12 on page 142. In this story, differentiate between the God-imposed punishment and David's self-imposed penance.

   If David had been your pastor, how would your church have handled the situation?

7. Read the comments by the parishioner and the former fan on pages 144 and 146. If the church were more "godly," would it more quickly "forgive and forget" the sins of its leaders and let them continue to serve even after they've sinned?

   What Bible passage would you cite to support the removal from leadership of a person who was openly sinning? What Bible passage would you cite to support allowing a leader who had openly sinned to keep his or her position?

8. When leaders fall publicly, there seems to be an invisible "time penance" that the church imposes on them, even if they do not take it up on their own. List several offenses, and give your opinion on how long people who have committed them should be "out of the loop" before they can be restored to leadership. What would be your "sentencing guidelines"? When finished, list the assumptions that were behind your opinions.

9. What will you do to begin practicing penance this week?

Chapter 14: Response

1. Read the quote by Richard Bach on page 159. Give several examples from your own experiences of how blessing and disaster exchanged places.

   What are the three primary blessings in your life, and how might they be used for evil if responded to wrongly?

   What is the greatest difficulty in your life and how might it be used for good if responded to rightly?

2. Refer to the scripture from James 1 on page 151. Do you think you could truly consider any trial that may come your way a "pure joy"?

   How does this scripture treat the relationship between character and circumstances differently than the world does?

3. Read 2 Corinthians 12:8–10 (page 153). We do not know what Paul's "thorn" may have been, but take a guess. List at least three possibilities.

   Examine the notion of "strength in weakness" by recalling Bible stories that illustrate this idea.

   Paul delighted in weakness because it made him rely on Christ. To what extent does our personal strength detract from our reliance on Christ? In what ways can a church be strong yet fail to rely on Christ?

4. Read 1 Peter 1:6–7 (page 152). Gold is refined by fire, but even gold will eventually perish. Yet our faith remains. Discuss why we value the tangible things of earth more than we value character and faith, which last for eternity. How can Christians come to value character, faith, and heaven more? What must change if we are to do so?

5. What will you do to begin practicing response this week?